W9-BWB-392

DATE DUE

EVALUATOR INTERVENTIONS
Pros and Cons

Volume 2
Sage Research Progress Series in Evaluation

SAGE RESEARCH PROGRESS SERIES IN EVALUATION

General Editor: SUSAN E. SALASIN, *National Institute of Mental Health*
Co-Editor (1979): ROBERT PERLOFF, *University of Pittsburgh*

EDITORIAL REVIEW BOARD

The Series Editors and the Publishers are grateful to those Board members who
refereed this year's volumes.

SAGE RESEARCH PROGRESS SERIES IN EVALUATION
Volume 2

Edited by
ROBERT PERLOFF

EVALUATOR INTERVENTIONS
Pros and Cons

Published in cooperation with the
EVALUATION RESEARCH SOCIETY

 **SAGE** PUBLICATIONS   Beverly Hills   London

H
62
.E87

For information address:

SAGE Publications, Inc.
275 South Beverly Drive
Beverly Hills, California 90212

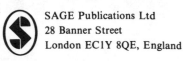

SAGE Publications Ltd
28 Banner Street
London EC1Y 8QE, England

Printed in the United States of America

Library of Congress Cataloging in Publication Data
Main entry under title:

Evaluator interventions.

    (Sage research progress series in evaluation ; v. 2)
    "Published in cooperation with the Evaluation
Research Society."
    Includes bibliographical references.
    1. Evaluation research (Social action programs)—
Addresses, essays, lectures. I. Perloff, Robert.
II. Evaluation Research Society. III. Series.
H62.E87   309   79-21481
ISBN 0-8039-1196-3
ISBN 0-8039-1197-1 pbk.

FIRST PRINTING

Contents

ABOUT THIS SERIES

The SAGE RESEARCH PROGRESS SERIES IN EVALUATION is a series of concisely edited works designed to present notable, previously unpublished writing on topics of current concern to the evaluation community. In keeping with a vision of evaluation as a methodological enterprise with outcomes at both the policy-making and services delivery levels, the series is designed to present state-of-the-art volumes for use by instructors and students of evaluation, researchers, practitioners, policy-makers, and program administrators.

Each volume (4 to 6 new titles will be published in each calendar year) focuses on themes which emerge from the previous year's annual meeting of the Evaluation Research Society—revised and supplemented by specially commissioned works.

The series begins in 1979 with five volumes, largely selected from papers delivered at the 2nd Annual Meeting of the Evaluation Research Society held in Washington, D.C. on November 2-4, 1978. The volumes in this inaugural year include:

QUALITATIVE AND QUANTITATIVE METHODS IN EVALUATION RESEARCH, edited by Thomas D. Cook and Charles S. Reichardt

EVALUATOR INTERVENTIONS: Pros and Cons, edited by Robert Perloff

TRANSLATING EVALUATION INTO POLICY, edited by Robert F. Rich

THE EVALUATOR AND MANAGEMENT, edited by Herbert C. Schulberg and Jeanette M. Jerrell

EVALUATION IN LEGISLATION, edited by Franklin M. Zweig

We are pleased that these initial volumes in the *SAGE RESEARCH PROGRESS SERIES IN EVALUATION* so well represent significant interdisciplinary contributions to the literature. Comments and suggestions from our readers will be welcomed.

SERIES EDITORS:

Susan E. Salasin, National Institute of Mental Health

Robert Perloff, University of Pittsburgh

ACKNOWLEDGMENTS

The editor and authors of the papers which follow express their deep appreciation to Dr. Norman Gold, National Institute of Education, for his invaluable guidance administratively and technically for the research and consultative activities which inspired the preparation of the papers appearing in this volume. Without his support, counsel, and encouragement, this volume would not have been possible.

The preparation of these chapters was supported in large part by a grant from the National Institute of Education to the Evaluation Research Society, Grant No. G-77-0069, for which the editor and authors are indeed thankful. The opinions expressed here are those of the authors and do not necessarily reflect the opinions or policies of the National Institute of Education.

Gratitude is also expressed to the Graduate School of Business, University of Pittsburgh, for its support in connection with a subcontract with the Evaluation Research Society, for administering the above grant, and to Ms. Margaret Jonnet of the Graduate School of Business, for her excellent assistance in the typing of manuscripts and for her logistical support.

This acknowledgment of indebtedness to sources of help in the preparation of this book would be conspicuously and thoughtlessly incomplete were it to be bereft of mention of three other persons whose contributions were enormous. I refer, first, to Sara Miller McCune, Publisher and President of Sage Publications, Inc., for her nearly boundless energies and skills as a publisher, and for her unfailing support of the enterprise of evaluation research and of the organization under whose aegis, essentially, this book was stimulated and brought to fruition, the

Evaluation Research Society. Next, there is Susan Salasin, General Series Editor, friend, colleague, gentle but firm and effective prodder, humanist, and one who cares and feels deeply about people in pain and about evaluation and knowledge utilization technology. Finally, there is my wife, Evelyn, who, if the truth were known, is much more knowledgeable about evaluation than am I, and who allowed me—though at times reluctantly!—to do my thing, one of the outgrowths of which is this book; her support and love, not to mention her wise counsel as an evaluator par excellence, were and continue to be invaluable.

Pittsburgh   *Robert Perloff*

Robert Perloff

EDITOR'S INTRODUCTION
Issues in Evaluation and Decision-Making

When all is said and done, the major purpose of an evaluation of an activity or program is to provide as rational and as comprehensive as possible a basis for making decisions vis-à-vis program formulation or adoption, changes, or dissolution. However, problems associated with improving the contribution of evaluative information to decision-making continue to be among the more complex facing the evaluation researcher. Though considerable energies are now being expended by evaluation researchers to deal with these important issues of utility, continued efforts directed at improving the usefulness of evaluative information for decision-making must be aggressively pursued. The chapters in this volume present both conceptual and methodological approaches designed to maximize the contribution of evaluative studies for various levels of decision-making.

The first article, by Ward Edwards, describes an intriguing and complex effort to evaluate a variety of school desegregation plans in Los Angeles. If any evidence were needed to document the relevance of evaluation research for significant and pervasive

EDITOR'S NOTE: *The opinions expressed in this introduction and in the other contributions to this volume are those of the authors and do not necessarily reflect the opinions or policies of the National Institute of Education.*

social problem decision-making, one need go no further than this fascinating case history of the role that multiattribute utility measurement can play in helping to resolve conflicts and to make decisions involving millions of dollars and the future lives of hundreds of thousands of young people. The procedure that Edwards describes is no less valid for a multitude of other huge social and educational programs than it is for school desegregation. In addition to the technical elegance of the quantitative model that Edwards espouses, the reader's attention is also invited to the care and success with which he sought and received the participation of a number of community stakeholders in developing the value tree central to the determination of the benefits ascribed to the various desegregation plans assessed via the Value Analysis System used to identify and weight these benefits. It is important to recognize that this procedure is one which the evaluation researcher may use before a program is initiated, to help determine how a heterogeneity of constituencies feel about various program alternatives. In this way, all parties involved are generally assured that their views are reasonably, accurately and comprehensively reflected in a plan or blueprint before it becomes operational. In turn, this process reduces the likelihood that grievances, demurrals, or disruptions will arise *after* a program is in place.

In his chapter on the responsibility for validating representations, Robert Stake does yeoman's service along many dimensions, not the least of which is in making essential and lucid distinctions between the objectives and responsibilities of two sets of decision-makers: program specialists, administrators, funding agents, and various elements of the general public; and evaluation specialists. (It should be noted at this juncture that, in the context of a particular case, Robert Perloff makes a similar point in his, the final paper in this volume.)

Stake is not so naive as to expect that it is totally possible for an evaluator to distinguish beween his or her role (a) as a more or less dispassionate evaluator and (b) as an individual with an ax to grind with respect to a particular program or social problem. Clearly, even though one wears two hats, both hats are on the same head. What Stake argues for is the ethical responsibility for the evaluator, *qua evaluator,* to strive to separate his function as a data gatherer and, if you will, a searcher for truth, from his or her sentiments and values about a particular social agenda.

Let it be made very clear that there are those who disagree with Stake's (and my own) position in this matter, but it is his view (and mine) that, to use his own words, "it is unethical to help improve the decision-making function, especially to make it more explicit and less intuitive, if accomplished under the guise of an evaluation service."

Perhaps the most important moral to be inferred from Stake's discourse is that program development, program operation, program evaluation, and program utilization are the responsibility of many sources of specialization, knowledge, and political sensitivity, wherein the evaluator is but one contributor to this mixed and frequently untidy constellation of inputs. When the evaluator brashly trespasses domains other than evaluation per se, he or she may, in Stake's terms, "contribute in a small way to the technologizing and disintegration of our society." Perhaps, he opines, this "is a small flaw in the social fabric. But it is our flaw, and our ethical standards should help us mend it." Amen.

Thus far we have addressed the evaluator's influence on decision-making prior to program operationalization (Edwards) and during the evaluation process itself (Stake). In the third chapter, by Thomas J. Kiresuk and Sander H. Lund, considerations are brought to bear upon decision-making following the evaluation of a specified program, that is, decisions crucial for judging whether and how the results of an evaluation should be integrated into the world beyond evaluation, into something called knowledge utilization.

These authors show how evaluation plays a role in facilitating the knowledge utilization process; conversely, they point out how knowledge utilization principles and procedures influence the evaluation process.

Speaking about the pros and cons of intervention, it may not be inappropriate to suggest that perhaps the only place where the evaluator has an obligation to intrude is at that point in a program's life cycle, when the evaluation is complete, at that point when the data are in, an experimental program has been assessed and found to be wanting or meritorious (probably both), and when the decision is made as to what should be done next. How shall the results of the program be implemented?

The final chapter (mine) in this collection is a suggestion of the costs and benefits which may be associated with the evaluator's unabashed intervention in a program he or she has undertaken to evaluate. While the case can certainly be made that certain circumstances justify evaluator intrusion, the proposition is advanced in this paper that the perils concomitant with such intrusion may, in some cases, outweigh the benefits.

So what are we able to conclude about evaluator intervention into an on-going program? Should evaluators have the "courage of their conviction" and plunge in "where fools fear to tread" or should they, rather (continuing with this cliche-ridden sentence), avoid intervention "like the plague"?

Unlike the consequences of many—perhaps most—intellectual forums and academic exercises, I believe we can say something concrete as a consequence of this volume. The advantages and appropriateness of intervention (the "pro" side, if you will) would appear to be fairly positive and unequivocal where we have the tools (multiattribute utility measurement and Decision Determinants Analysis, for example) and at points in time when we may well be viewed as being more helpful (although Stake may not agree with this so far as the Los Angeles desegregation study is concerned) than harmful. The "points in time" to which I refer are those before a study begins (Edwards) and, to some extent, after a study has been terminated and knowledge transfer might begin (Kiresuk and Lund). Where the waters are somewhat murky is where we are concerned with intervention with respect to an evaluation *in process*. As is pointed out in the chapters by Stake and Perloff, there may well be risks, but then again from the point of view of the *formative* evaluation benefits that might accrue to a program from responsible and limited—*but always documented*—evaluator intervention, perhaps there are occasions when such intervention should be sanctioned. You pays your money and takes your choice!

Ward Edwards
Social Science Research Institute
University of Southern California

1

MULTIATTRIBUTE UTILITY MEASUREMENT
Evaluating Desegregation Plans in a Highly Political Context

INTRODUCTION

In August of 1963, Mary Ellen Crawford, a Black student living in Watts, filed a suit in Superior Court claiming that the Los Angeles Board of Education was violating her constitutional rights in that her school was segregated. More accurately, lawyers employed by the NAACP and the ACLU filed the suit on her behalf. These two organizations provided legal talent and support throughout the 15-year-long history of this still unfinished case; throughout the remainder of this chapter, when I write "the plaintiffs" I will be referring to them or their legal representatives. The suit did not claim deliberate discrimination; the problem was one of de facto segregation resulting from the geographical inhomogeneity of racial distribution over the vast, sprawling Los Angeles Unified School District.

The case had a long, complex legal history. The Superior Court found in 1970 that the District was indeed violating Mary Ellen Crawford's rights, and ordered it to desegregate. In 1975, that decision was reversed on appeal by the Court of Appeals, and the Court of Appeals was in turn reversed by the California Supreme Court in June, 1976. The California Supreme Court found that Mary Ellen Crawford's rights under the Constitution of the State of California, not the U.S. Constitution, had been violated, so their decision was treated as final. On June 28, 1976, the California Supreme Court ordered the District to desegregate. The nature of the order was inevitably relatively general. A key quote from it ordered that the Board "immediately prepare and implement a reasonably feasible desegregation plan."

Thus reasonableness and feasibility became the ultimate test against which any integration plan was to be measured, but the terms are deliberately vague. All legal action taken since then can be interpreted as attempts to apply the test to the process of planning and carrying out the process of desegregation.

The California Supreme Court decision directed that a Superior Court Judge be appointed to monitor and supervise both planning and execution of the process of desegregating LAUSD—a monumental task indeed. Judge Paul Egly was appointed. Subject to various kinds of potential appeals (none of which have as yet occurred as this is written) this made Judge Egly the ultimate arbiter responsible for evaluation of both planning and execution of this enormous task. Ultimately (subject to appeal) he decides what "reasonable and feasible" means, and whether plans and their execution do or do not meet this vaguely worded mandate.

One of the early problems with which Judge Egly had to deal was petitions from interested groups of Los Angeles citizens to become intervenors in the case. (An intervenor, while not a plaintiff or defendant, has a legal standing in a case, in that he or it can be represented by counsel in all court proceedings, can initiate some kinds of legal actions bearing on the issue at hand, and plays a major public role. This is appropriate, since the function of intervenors in cases like this is to help represent, within the legal framework of the case, the viewpoints of broad but differing segments of public opinion.)

Ultimately, four organizations were admitted as intervenors: Citizens' Advisory Committee on Student Integration (CACSI), Better Education for Students Today (BEST), BUSTOP, and The Integration Project. CACSI as an intervenor organization grew (or, more accurately, shrank) out of a major citizens' committee appointed by the District in 1976, to advise it about integration policy. That committee prepared both guidelines and a fairly detailed plan for integrating LAUSD and submitted them to the Board in early 1977. The Board adopted a less sweeping plan of its own; thereafter, elements of CACSI modified themselves into an intervenor group. The names of the other three organizations roughly indicate the primary focus of their different concerns. All were, and are, committed to the ideal of educational excellence. But they represent quite different views of what constitutes an excellent education, and how to go about creating it. They also make different interpretations of the California Supreme Court's phrase "reasonable and feasible."

On March 3, 1977 the Board submitted to Judge Egly a plan for desegregating the District, identified in Court and in this chapter as Exhibit A. It included the CACSI plan as an appendix, but was considerably less sweeping. On July 5, 1977, Judge Egly issued a Minute Order finding that the Board plan was insufficient. It directed the Board to present within 90 days a plan or plans that would realistically commence the desegregation of the district no later than February, 1978, to consider all reasonable alternative plans, to accompany and support its plan or plans and the alternatives by detailed findings and conclusions,

> including all evidentiary data; summaries of the opinions of experts' studies, both staff and outside, all statistical information; all cost and benefit studies; all financial information; all educational benefits and detriments; and any and all information developed either in support of its final plan or plans or used in evaluating the alternative plans.
>
> ... The Board and its staff shall give to the designated representatives of the petitioners and all intervenors (in Crawford) all reasonable access to the Board and its staff's planning process and data.

Responding to the evaluative part of this requirement, a group of senior staff members of the Los Angeles Unified School District led by Dr. Thomas O. Lawson, Director for Special Projects, and Mr. George E. McMullen, Budget Director, set out to devise a method of assembling the analytic and evaluative information required. I entered the process at an early stage, remained associated with it throughout design and execution phases and wrote the report that was submitted to Judge Egly. This chapter is essentially a summary of that report, along with some technical discussion of issues inherent in it, but not treated there, and some reporting on the aftermath.

It is worth pointing out the awesome difficulties of desegregating the Los Angeles Unified School District. The District is huge; in 1976 it included 559 schools and about 600,000 pupils. It sprawls. The maximum linear distance from one end to the other is 58 miles. Freeway distances are longer. Unlike most school districts that are ordered to desegregate, it is for most practical purposes quadriracial. In our demographic complications we found it necessary to classify its pupils into Blacks, Hispanic-Americans, Asian-Americans and other minorities, and Other Whites. In the early 1980s Hispanic-Americans will constitute more than 50% of the LAUSD pupil population. Blacks and Other Whites, both decreasing in number and percentage, will be about 20% each. The remaining 10% will be Asian-Americans and other minorities. (These demographic projections do not take into account any changes that might be produced by a desegregation plan.) Considerable amounts of instruction occur (and must occur) in Los Angeles schools in languages other than English.

The District, though it extends from the San Fernando Valley to San Pedro, does not include many areas that most would think a part of Los Angeles. Among the areas excluded are: Santa Monica, Beverly Hills, Culver City, Burbank, Glendale, Inglewood, Pasadena, Palos Verdes, Torrance and Compton. Some of these areas are overwhelmingly White. Except perhaps for Pasadena, all would make geographical sense as parts of the District. Their noninclusion is the result of long-standing political boundaries, and was never an overt issue in the case.

The San Fernando Valley contains many Other Whites. Eastern Los Angeles, as much as an hour away by freeway at 55 mph, contains a highly concentrated population of Hispanic-Americans. Blacks are heavily concentrated in South Central Los

Angeles, also about an hour by freeway from the Valley in non-rush hours.

Those are a few of the parameters of the problem that District desegregation planners, and external planners, had to face.

No planner in the District seriously considered a Metropolitan plan, i.e., a plan that would include non-District pupils. Only one external plan was of that type (and the evaluation scheme described here was not applied to it). Those in a position to know told me that any Metropolitan plan would delay desegregation, because of legal battles, for at least ten more years.

PROBLEM

Los Angeles Unified School District (LAUSD) required a method that would enable it to compare and evaluate all proposed desegregation/integration plans submitted to it as a result of Judge Egly's Minute Order uniformly and fairly. The method had to be encompassing enough to capture the plans, simple enough to be easily communicable, and had to permit comparisons of one plan with another both at relatively high levels of aggregation and in greater detail. It also had to differentiate sharply between description and analysis, on the one hand, and evaluation, on the other. If possible, it should also define "a good plan" to aid plan writers in preparing one.

I proposed to Dr. Lawson and Mr. McMullen (and, later, to other members of the Superintendent's Executive Team for Student Integration) that a version of multiattribute utility measurement would permit measurement of the benefits of each integration plan. After discussion, the proposal was accepted. Since multiattribute utility measurement is too technical a name, it was called the Value Analysis System (VAS). It explicitly treated only benefits. Monetary costs were calculated, at least to a first approximation, by a relatively simple procedure that Mr. McMullen had previously devised. For the most part, District budget experts made cost calculations on the basis of information provided by those preparing plans. The benefit analysis included nonmonetary costs; reduction of time on the bus or of organization difficulties produced by hiring new teachers or transferring those already hired can be thought of as benefits.

METHOD

Defining the Value Tree

The first step in any multiattribute analysis is to identify the decision-maker(s). In this case the Board made the decisions subject to court review. The second step is to define what dimensions of value are important enough to consider. In a complex topic like school desegregation, such dimensions of value will be hierarchically arranged. The first requirement of VAS was to identify the elements of this hierarchy and to determine its structure. We called the result the value tree.

Dr. Lawson, Mr. McMullen, and I prepared a value tree, with the aid of several other members of the LAUSD staff. It was, inevitably, excessively complex. We presented it to members of the Board of Education, and to representatives of the plaintiffs and intervenors. Their comments led us to add several further value dimensions, but not to restructure the tree and certainly not to reduce its complexity. In fact, we spent much effort resisting suggestions that would have made it more complex. The final version of the tree, discussed here, was the eighth we prepared.

The value tree arranges a series of elements in a structure. Unfortunately, there is no way to combine elements and structure in a single page display. Consequently, Figure 1 shows the structure only. The letters inside Figure 1 refer to the particular values included in the tree, and are described (in less than full detail) in the text that follows Figure 1.

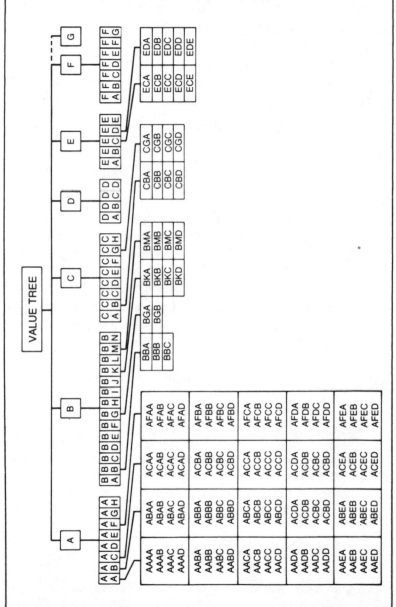

Figure 1.

19

THE VALUE TREE, MODEL 8

A. Effect of a segregation plan on racial-ethnic compositions.

B. Effect of a desegregation plan on educational quality.

C. Community acceptance of a desegregation plan.

D. Implications of a desegregation plan for District personnel.

E. Destabilizing effects of a desegregation plan.

F. Provisions within a desegregation plan for monitoring and evaluation.

AA. Racial-ethnic proportions of pupils moved from local schools.

AB. Racial-ethnic proportions in resulting schools.

AC. Racial-ethnic proportions of pupils bused. (Note: originally we expected some nonbusing plans. None were submitted, so this branch was treated like AA.)

AD. Number of grades affected by reassignments.

AE. Duration in weeks of integrated educational experience.

AF. Numbers of students remaining in isolated schools.

AG. Provisions for reduction of racial-ethnic isolation in still-segregated schools.

AH. Provisions for effectively preventing the resegregation of integrated schools.

AAA, AAB, AAC, AAD, AAE. These are proportions of pupils moved from local schools broken up by grade levels. AAA refers to Kindergarten; AAB refers to grades 1-3; AAC refers to grades 4-6; AAD refers to 7-9; AAE refers to 10-12. These are all further partitioned below.

AAAA, AAAB, AAAC, AAAD. These refer to proportions of Kindergarten pupils moved from local schools who are Black, Hispanic-American, Other White, and Asian-American and other minority, respectively.

––––––

AABA through AAED. These are like AAAA-AAAD in all respects except that different grade levels are referred to.

––––––

ABA, ABB, ABC, ABD, ABE. These are racial-ethnic proportions of pupils in resulting schools broken up by grade levels, in the same manner as for AAA-AAE. They are all further partitioned below.

––––––

ABAA through ABED. These are like AAAA through AAED except that they refer to racial-ethnic proportions in resulting schools instead of among those moved.

––––––

ACA, ACB, ACC, ACD, ACE. These are racial-ethnic proportions of pupils bused broken up by grade levels, in the same manner as for AAA-AAE. They are all further partitioned below.

––––––

ACAA through ACED. These are like AAAA through AAED except that they refer to racial-ethnic proportions within grade levels among pupils bused instead of among those moved.

––––––

AFA, AFB, AFC, AFD, AFE. These are numbers of students remaining in racially or ethnically isolated schools broken up by grade levels, in the same manner as for AAA-AAE. They are all further partitioned below.

––––––

AFAA through AFED. These are numbers of students remaining in racially or ethnically isolated schools broken up by grade levels and by racial-ethnic category.

BA. Impact of a plan on student-teacher ratios.

BB. Impact of a plan on classroom heterogeneity.

BC. Impact of a plan on staff attitudes.

BD. Impact of a plan on student attitudes.

BE. Impact of a plan on learning of basics.

BF. Impact of a plan on participation of volunteers.

BG. Impact of a plan on availability of pupil options.

BH. Impact of a plan on average teacher-student contact hours per day.

BI. Impact of a plan on availability of multicultural education.

BJ. Impact of a plan on teacher quality.

BK. Impact of a plan on adequacy and use of facilities.

BL. Impact of a plan on identification of pupils with their home schools. (Home school does not necessarily mean neighborhood school. It means the school which the pupil is regularly assigned.)

BM. Availability of special programs for pupils with special needs.

BN. Impact of a plan on learning of interracial and interethnic acceptance.

BBA. Impact of a plan on socio-economic heterogeneity.

BBB. Impact of a plan on heterogeneity of past educational achievement.

BBC. Impact of a plan on heterogeneity of lingual skills.

BGA. Impact of a plan on pupil curricular options.

BGB. Impact of a plan on pupil extracurricular options.

BKA. Impact of a plan on needs for double and short sessions.

BKB. Impact of a plan on reduction of concentration of pupils at high-density schools.

BKC. Provision within a plan for reduction of maintenance backlog.

BKD. Extent to which space is available for new facilities required by a plan.

_____

BMA. Availability of special programs for beginning learners.

BMB. Availability of special programs for educationally disadvantged pupils (Title 1, SB 90).

BMC. Availability of special programs for gifted pupils.

BMD. Availability of special programs for bilingual and bicultural pupils.

_____

CA. Effect of a plan on parent, community member, teacher, and participation in local school decision making.

CB. Effect of a plan on parental attitudes.

CC. Effect of a plan on the attitudes of opinion leaders.

CD. Effect of a plan on pressure group attitudes.

CE. Effect of a plan on the attitudes of political leaders.

CF. Effect of a plan on the media.

CG. Effect of a plan on producing or avoiding family flight.

CH. Existence within a plan of explicit provisions and plans for enhancing community acceptance.

_____

CBA. Effect of a plan on attitudes of Black parents.

CBB. Effect of a plan on attitudes of Hispanic-American parents.

CBC. Effect of a plan on attitudes of Other White parents.

CBD. Effect of a plan on attitudes of Asian-American or other minority parents.

CGA. Impact of a plan on producing or avoiding flight of Black families from LAUSD.

CGB. Impact of a plan on producing or avoiding flight of Hispanic-American families from LAUSD.

CGC. Impact of a plan on producing or avoiding flight of Other White families.

CGD. Impact of a plan on producing or avoiding flight of Asian-American or other minority families.

DA. Implications of a desegregation plan for new hires of District personnel.

DB. Implications of a plan for transfers or relocation of District personnel.

DC. Implications of a plan for teacher and other staff development.

DD. Impact of a plan on maintenance of harmonious employee-employer relations with the District.

EA. Number of additional classrooms required.

EB. Planning for phase-in of plan.

EC. Number of students bused.

ED. Average amount of time per bused pupil per day spent riding buses.

EE. Effect of a desegregation plan on the safety of pupils, teachers, and facilities and equipment.

ECA. Number of kindergarten students bused.

ECB, ECC, ECD, ECE. Like ECA except that they refer to grades 1-3, 4-6, 7-9, and 10-12 respectively.

EDA through EDE. These are average amounts of time per bused pupil per day spent riding buses, broken down by the five grade categories.

FA. Provisions within a plan for monitoring and evaluating racial-ethnic compositions.

FB. Provisions within a plan for monitoring and evaluating educational quality.

FC. Provisions within a plan for monitoring and evaluating community acceptance.

FD. Provisions within a plan for monitoring and evaluating implications for District personnel.

FE. Provisions within a plan for monitoring and evaluating destabilizing effects.

FF. Provisions within a plan for monitoring and evaluating the monitoring and evaluation system itself.

FG. Provisions within a plan for monitoring and evaluating its financial implications.

We made available to all respondents, interested parties, and the media a full tree structure presentation of the value tree, with values labeled. It took a large piece of paper.

From a technical point of view the value tree is far too complex, and the financial and human costs of working with it were substantial. It has 144 twigs (bottom locations on the tree), each requiring a weight and a set of single-division utilities. (These are technical terms from decision theory. Explanations of their meaning and elicitation come later in this paper.) Yet in this highly controversial and political context, I doubt that any of its structure could have been omitted. All of the issues contained within it are in fact relevant to the merits of desegregation plans. For example, the tree could have been much simpler if it had not, in those branches concerned with racial-ethnic composition, treated five different grade groupings separately, or if it had treated fewer than four racial-ethnic categories. The demographic problems of so fine a breakdown were enormous, and in fact the solutions we used for them were appropriate and unsatisfactory. Yet we could not work with fewer racial-ethnic categories (and indeed we had to resist some minor pressures to add more). The grade groupings were also essential; in fact, their presence led to some of the most useful consequences of the effort. The cost and technical unsatisfactoriness of so complex a structure were more than offset by political necessity.

Members of the Board and representatives of plaintiffs and intervenors considered the initial version of the value tree very complex and hard to understand. Yet no one proposed simplification. Most of those who took the time and effort to study it in detail came to accept it as inevitable, and objected to it only because its complexity made it difficult and unwieldy to use and understand. The only modifications were additions of value dimensions we had failed to include originally. An example was AH, provisions for preventing the resegregation of integrated schools. Some of these, as it turned out, were quite important; their original omission had represented intellectual lapses on our parts, presumably resulting at least in part from the incredible time pressure under which we were working. (The entire study reported here took two months; including not only formal but persuasive and computational tasks, and writing; 14-hour days and 7-day weeks were routine.)

Given the value tree, in final form, the next problem was how to proceed with the evaluation. The sophisticated elicitation procedures proposed by Keeney and Raiffa (1976) were obviously unsuited to this situation. There were many respondents; data had to be collected quickly from busy people having no time to learn more than the most elementary procedures. The basic ideas of SMART (Edwards, 1972, 1977; Gardiner and Edwards, 1975), were appropriate—but even they required simplification.

SMART uses a linear model to combine weights representing the importance of each dimension of evaluation with the single-dimension utility appropriate to that dimension, for each object of evaluation. A great deal of evidence (e.g., Dawes and Corrigan,

1974; Yntema and Torgerson, 1961; Edwards and von Winter-feldt, 1973a, 1973b, 1973c) shows that linear models are good approximations to more complex and sophisticated aggregation rules. In any case, complex and sophisticated aggregation rules were inappropriate to the application, since one of its require-ments was reasonable transparency to those not trained in mathe-matical thinking or decision analysis.

We needed still another simplification. We could not use com-plex or sophisticated procedures to elicit single dimension utilities. Some dimensions, such as "AG. Provisions for reduction of racial-ethnic isolation in still-segregated schools" are clearly judgmental. An expert, familiar with a plan, could simply judge its performance on this dimension on a 1-100 scale. Other dimen-sions were objective. We chose to treat all transformation from objective measures to utilities as linear or triangular. Those for which more is better than less (e.g., number of grades involved in an integration plan) were defined by specifying the minimum value (0, in the example) as 0, the maximum value (13) as 100, and drawing a straight line between them. Similarly, those for which less is better than more (e.g., time on the bus) were defined as lines with negative rather than positive slope (in that example, the minimum, 0 minutes, has utility 100 and the maximum, 180 minutes, has utility 0). Finally, some dimensions have interior maxima. The most obvious is racial-ethnic compositions; either 0% or 100% of any one race in a school was defined as having utility zero, while a percentage equal to the percentage of that racial-ethnic group in the District as a whole was defined to have utility 100. Thus every single dimension utility function was one of four types, and the objective ones were specified by either two or three numbers. We carefully explained this to all respondents, both verbally and in detailed written instructions, and every response form carried the relevant information (measurement or judgment, and the two or three relevant measurement para-meters if appropriate) on the form, so that the respondent would be reminded of them as he or she responded.

The notion of importance weight was also carefully defined, for those who had to make such judgments. We emphasized heavily the concept of tradeoffs, especially as distinguished from cutoffs, in both written and verbal explanations. All instructions made clear that the task of judging single dimension utilities is essentially a technical one, to be performed by LAUSD experts— different experts for different dimensions. The task of judging importance weights, on the other hand, is clearly the essence of value judgments, and should be done, if possible, by members of the Board, and by parties to the case. (We did not consider the possibility that others might disagree with us about the shape of any utility function—and in fact no one ever questioned any judgment of that sort that we had made.)

But obtaining importance weights for 144 values is an impossible judgmental task, if done directly. So we used an indirect procedure. Each respondent who judged importance weights did so for each level of the tree separately. The first page of the response booklet for importance weights compared values A, B, C, D, E, and F. The second page compared AA, AB, AC, AD, AE, AF, AG, AH, and so on. The method of collecting these judgments is described below; at the moment, the point is only that each weighter produced a set of weights summing to 1 within each set of values appearing on one page of the response booklet.

Response sheets for all values below the highest level of the hierarchy had two columns, one labeled "Normalized Weights" (NW) and the other "Final Weights" (FW). The normalized weights are described in the previous paragraph. The final weights are obtained by multiplication downward, for all but the top level of the hierarchy. Thus, $FW(AAAA) = NW(AAAA) \times FW(AAA) = NW(AAAA) \times NW(AAA) \times NW(AA) \times NW(A)$. Thus, the final weights at the bottom of the value tree sum to 1 over the whole tree.

Given the single-dimension utilities for each of the twigs (bottom locations on the value tree), and final weights that sum to 1 over the whole tree, it is easy to apply the standard linear formula; multiply utilities times weights and add these products over twigs. A sum over all twigs will give an aggregate benefit measure for the whole plan. A profile of any plan's performance on each major value (or values lower in the hierarchy) gives more useful information. It shows what values are well served and what values are less well served by a particular plan. To obtain such a profile, first sum products of utility times final weights for all twigs dependent on the value to be included in the profile. Then divide by the final weight of that value. In symbols, if $u(t_i)$ is the single-dimension utility of the ith twig and $u(V_j)$ is the desired summary value, then for a given plan:

$$u(V_j) = \sum_{t_i \in V_j} FW(t_i) \, u(t_i) / FW(V_j),$$

where $t_i \in V_j$ means that the summation should extend only over twigs dependent on (connected with and lower in the hierarchy than) V_j. The division by $FW(V_j)$ simply puts all such subsummaries on the same 0-100 scale, to make them easier to understand and compare.

We did not handle financial costs in this way. In spite of the usual pitfalls of such numbers, benefit-to-cost ratios seemed useful, since we saw no method of expressing these abstract benefit measures in units that would make them comparable to dollars. But of course such ratios require that both benefits and costs have an origin. We chose to define zero benefit as the benefit obtained, using the value tree and weights, from operating LAUSD in 1976-1977. Similarly, zero cost was the cost of that year's operation. These numbers were subtracted from the benefit and cost numbers for each plan for subsequent years, and the resulting differences were used as numerator and denominator of a benefit-to-cost ratio.

We wanted, if possible, to obtain at least a five-year forward projection of the benefits and costs of each plan. We did in fact obtain such judgments. But to reduce computation time (since we were facing an inflexible deadline) and because there was too much detail in the information already, we actually used only the figures for 1978-1979, the presumed and actual first year of operation of the chosen plan, and for 1981-1982, when the plan should have established itself and be free of start-up problems.

We considered, without much success, the question of what to do if benefit/cost ratios favored one plan while benefits favored another. Fortunately, this didn't happen.

Eliciting Importance Weights

The touchiest, most difficult part of the whole process was that of eliciting importance weights. These weights, the essence of value judgments, were essential. But the situation was highly political, and it is difficult to imagine a member of the Board of Education, for example, expressing his or her views in public, or in a document that was to be part of a court record, concerning the relative numerical importance of educational quality and racial-ethnic composition.

We were eager to get as many relevant sets of weights as possible. While we were (correctly) convinced that we could not expect individual Board members to provide weights, we hoped that some kind of collective set of weights might be possible. So we proposed to each Board member that he or she fill out the 27 weighting sheets, in private. I was present to give instructions, answer questions, and check to make sure the respondent understood the procedure. These response forms were kept confidential. After all Board members willing to participate had completed the judgmental task, I averaged their weights, returned their original weighting sheets to them, and reported only the averages. Five of the seven Board members provided weights. (It may or may not be a coincidence that the two who did not provide weights were also the two who voted against the integration plan that the Board ultimately adopted.)

The numbers hereafter called "Board weights" are averages of those judged by the five participating Board members.

We also sought weights from representatives of each of the plaintiffs and intervenors. The plaintiffs refused to provide them, arguing that their primary responsibility was to evaluate the Board's ultimate plan, rather than external plans submitted for the Board's consideration. CACSI and the Integration Project also refused to provide them. CACSI seemed to feel that the system was complicated and biased, though details of their reasons for thinking it biased never became clear to me. The Integration Project objected to the fact that racial-ethnic composition and educational quality were treated as equivalent top-level values. They wished educational quality to be treated as a sub-category under racial-ethnic composition, on the argument that no segregated education can possess educational quality. We were unwilling to make that change in the structure of the value tree, so they were unwilling to provide weights.

BEST provided very carefully thought-out weights, which were used. BUSTOP also prepared weights, but too late to permit their use in final calculations.

Finally, I obtained weights from Robert J. Havighurst, Professor of Education and Human Development, University of Chicago, Professor Norman Miller, Department of Psychology and Social Science Research Institute, University of Southern California, and Dr. Neil Sullivan, former Superintendent of Schools, Berkeley, California, former Commissioner of Education, State of Massachusetts; all are experts on education and desegregation. I conducted each weight elicitation individually, in a face-to-face session lasting from one to four hours, with no interruptions permitted. The respondents began by reading seven pages of instruction and explanation, after which I answered any questions—of which there were usually many. A sample filled-in page of the response sheets was shown to each respondent and one is reproduced below.

E x a m p l e   P a g e

Response Sheet 1

Values to be judged

A. Impacts of a plan on racial-ethnic compositions.
B. Impacts of a plan on educational quality.
C. Impacts of a plan on community acceptance.
D. Impacts of a plan on District personnel.
E. Destabilizing aspects of a plan (e.g., phase-in, time on the bus, number bused, safety).
F. Monitoring and evaluation aspects of a plan.

Column Numbers

1 Values	2 Ratios	3 Ratios	4 Ratios	5 Ratios	6 Ratios	7 Normalized Weights
B	250	250	100	100	17	.532
A	150	150	60	60	10	.319
C	25	25	10	10		.053
E	25	25	10			.053
D	10	10				.021
F	10					.021
Sums	470					.999

Respondents first ranked the values in descending order of importance by entering the letter(s) designating the value in column 1. Ties were permitted. "Importance" was explained as follows, both in the instruction sheet pages and in verbal explanation:

> Weights are of course subjective; no two people are likely to agree about them. They represent the judged importance of each aspect of performance. Suppose, for example, you judge the importance of BE, learning of basics, to be twice that of BI, availability of multicultural education. This means that you would be willing to accept a 10% reduction in availability of multicultural education in order to obtain a 5% increase in learning of basics. All other importance weights mean the same sort of thing. It is their ratio properties, not their absolute levels, that count.
>
> In order to think about such trade-offs, you need to know what 0 and 100 mean for each dimension. 0 always means worst and 100 always means best, but you should know what points have been chosen as representing best and worst. We have tried to make sure that all plans will present values that fall within those ranges.

Instructions also explained the nature of single-dimension utility functions, explained for each twig which type (judgmental, increasing, decreasing, or triangular) it was, and, for the last three cases, gave the two, or in the case of triangular functions, three parameters that defined the function.

Next, respondents judged whether the lowest dimension in the rank order was completely irrelevant. If so, it received a 0 normalized weight and the respondent made all subsequent judgments in column 3 and above (or still shorter columns if more than one dimension was completely irrelevant). Such judgments did occur, though not often and not at the top of the value hierarchy.

The number 10 appeared at the lowest point in each column. Respondents made ratio judgments of the importance of each value relative to the least important one. (Ten rather than 1 was the starting point to permit ratios of less than 2:1 without need for decimals.) Of course ratios had no upper bound; some respondents used numbers in excess of 1000.

The respondent used column 2 first, unless he or she had judged some dimension to be utterly irrelevant; in that case the respondent used whichever column assigned 10 to the least important nonzero dimension and columns to the right of that one. Next, I told the respondent to ignore judgments in column 2, forget about the value dimension at the bottom of column 2, and make judgments as though the bottom value dimension in column 3 had been least important. At this point, I usually noticed inconsistences between ratios in columns 2 and 3. I brought these to the respondent's attention, and invited revision of any or all numbers so far assessed to bring about consistency. This often led to hard thought and the revision of many numbers. When all columns except the last were filled in, I quickly calculated the normalized weights from column 2. Only when the respondent was satisfied with all judgments and with the normalized weights did we go on to the next response sheet.

After three or four response sheets, some respondents felt it unnecessary to fill in all columns or started calculating ratios for themselves, or both. I encouraged use of as many columns as the respondent was willing to use. If the respondent's comments made me unsure that a particular ratio represented an appropriate measure of relative importance, I usually insisted that he or she fill in a column that would highlight the particular ratio I doubted—typically the column in which the less important value in that ratio was assigned 10. Whenever possible I insisted on calculating normalized weights before leaving the response sheet, so the respondent could look at his other judgments in at least two different but logically equivalent ways. (A hand-held calculator does such arithmetic very rapidly.)

Respondents were in almost every case thoughtful and careful in their responses—often returning to earlier ones to reconsider and modify them. Though the task of ratio judgment is sometimes considered difficult by psychophysicists, I felt that all these unusual and sophisticated respondents understood it well. If not, as occasionally occurred, I worked through numerical examples until I was satisfied that the confusion, whatever it might be, had been cleared up.

Starting with Response Sheet 8, excluding 12, 13, 14, and 15, the judgments could, if the respondent wanted, be based on obvious logical rules. Each such sheet contained an explanation of the rule and a place in which the respondent could check a box to indicate that it should be used. For example, Response Sheet 8 was concerned with AAA-AAE, racial-ethnic proportions of pupils moved from local schools, stratified by the five grade groupings (K, 1-3, 4-6, 7-9, 10-12). It included two possible logical rules with boxes to be checked. One read:

> If you believe that all pupils, regardless of grade level, should be considered equally in assessing the merits of racial-ethnic mixes in proportions of pupils moved from local schools, check here and do not fill out the rest of this sheet. Staff will enter weights proportional to the number of pupils in each grade grouping in LAUSD.

The second box on Response Sheet 8 was like the first except that it permitted respondents to specify a grade level below which pupils should not be included in the calculation and entered 0 weights for grades below that. All boxes available to be checked on other sheets were based on similar ideas of equivalence among pupils of different ethnicity, grade level or both.

Many respondents used these boxes; some did not. For example, some respondents felt that certain ethnicities deserved especially high weight, and so preferred to judge ratios for themselves. Others felt similarly about grade groupings.

A special problem arose in the E branch, response sheet 6, concerned with destabilizing effects. All but one of these dimensions were undesirable; the more students bused, the worse, other things being equal. High importance meant that it was especially desirable to avoid this value, rather than to seek it out. I carefully monitored this change of interpretation of importance, explaining it when we turned to response sheet 6 and making sure from the content of the responses that each respondent understood it. Inter-respondent variation at all levels of the value tree was generally smaller than I had expected.

I had the opportunity to present, at a meeting of the Board of Education well prior to preparation of their own plans (and well prior to evaluation of plans prepared by others) a written and oral report of their own average weights. (Of course these averages are over normalized weights, not ratios.) The following quote from the written report summarizes these results and my interpretation of them.

> The Value Analysis System is designed to evaluate plans, not to write them. It is nevertheless appropriate to consider how one would go about writing a plan that would be likely to score high on it.
>
> It is important to emphasize that all weighters were told to assume that their weights are intended only to discriminate among Constitutionally acceptable plans. In other words, the weighting of the racial-ethnic compositions branch vis-a-vis the other branches is for the purpose of comparing plans, each of which is assumed to have a Constitutionally acceptable racial-ethnic character.
>
> Inspection of the averaged weights of the five participating Board members gives some rather clear ideas about how to write a plan that would serve well the values that the Board considers important. Although two Board members did not participate in the weighting, various considerations make it seem likely that if they had, the same conclusions would have been appropriate.
>
> First, consider Table 1, which shows the average Board weights for the single-letter values.

Table 1: Average Board Weights for Single-Letter Values

A.	Racial-ethnic Compositions	16%
B.	Educational Quality	40%
C.	Community Acceptance	23%
D.	Implications for District Personnel	8%
E.	Destabilizing Aspects	11%
F.	Monitoring and Evaluation	3%

Educational quality is overwhelmingly of most importance. Community acceptance comes next. Then comes racial-ethnic compositions. Destabilization effects get only 11%; the other values still less. At this level of generality, the message is clear but unsurprising: design an integration program meeting the requirements of *Crawford* that is of high educational quality and that engenders community acceptance; those issues are more important than details of racial-ethnic balances and problems of destabilization.

Under the heading of educational quality, what is important? Consider Table 2, which lists the first six values under educational quality.

Table 2: First Six Values Under Educational Quality

BE.	Impact on learning of basics	14%
BD.	Impact on student attitudes	13%
BJ.	Impact on teacher quality	10%
BL.	Impact on identification with home schools	9%
BA.	Impact on student-teacher ratios	9%
BM.	Impact on special programs	8%

The first message of Table 2 is that no single aspect of educational quality stands out strongly over the others; they tail off gently in importance. The fact that basics are most important carries a clear implication that they should be emphasized even at the expense of "enrichment" type programs. Issues of student attitudes and teacher quality are closely related and carry clear implications. A program that ensures that basics are well taught by skilled teachers to students who like the experience is sure to do well with respect to educational quality.

Under community acceptance, four values get most of the weight.

Table 3: First Four Values Under Community Acceptance

CH.	Existence in plan of explicit methods for enhancing community acceptance	24%
CG.	Effect on family flight	20%
CA.	Local participation in local decision making	18%
CB.	Effect on parental attitudes	15%

Obviously, the most important thing about community acceptance is to make explicit plans for obtaining it. It is obtained if family flight is avoided, if the plan provides for local parent, teacher, and community participation in local school decision making, and if the parents like it. Effects on media, on pressure groups, and on political leaders are far less important—and in any case probably derive from these primary effects.

Under racial-ethnic compositions, the weights tail off gently with no sharp breaks. The first four values are:

Table 4: First Four Values Under Racial-Ethnic Compositions

AB.	Racial-ethnic proportions in resulting classes	20%
AH.	Provisions for preventing resegregation	17%
AA.	Racial-ethnic proportions of pupils moved	14%
AD.	Number of grades affected by reassignments	13%

Obviously the effect on resulting classes is most important. Programmatic provisions for preventing resegregation comes next—in effect, it is most important to desegregate classes and to keep the pupils desegregated. Number of grades and fairness of which pupils ride the buses are also important.

Under destabilizing effects one issue, safety, is most important.

Table 5: Values Under Destabilizing Effects

EE.	Effect on safety	36%
EC.	Number of pupils bused	22%
EB.	Planning for phase-in of a plan	19%
ED.	Average amount of time per bused pupil spend riding buses	15%
DA.	Implications for number of additional classrooms	8%

Safety is crucial. Next comes number bused, which is meaningfully more important than the amount of time on the bus. Phase-in is also important.

Provided safety is adequately addressed, it is better from the standpoint of these values, to bus fewer pupils for longer times than vice versa.

By moving further down the Value Tree, we can also find out which pupils should be bused and which ones should not. Obviously, busing itself is undesirable; its only merit is that it is necessary in order to fulfill other values. Table 6 shows the relative undesirability of busing pupils of various grade groups.

Table 6: Undesirability of Busing Pupils by Grades

ECA.	Kindergarten	32%
ECB.	Grades 1-3	27%
ECE.	Grades 10-12	17%
ECD.	Grades 7-9	13%
ECC.	Grades 4-6	11%

In other words, it is almost three times as bad to bus a kindergarten child as a child in grades 4-6, and not much better to bus a child in grades 1-3 than a kindergarten child.

Issues having to do with District personnel and with monitoring and evaluation are not sufficiently important to deserve major attention, except as they have to do with teacher quality and teacher-pupil ratios.

In sum, these weights call for a plan that:

a. meets the mandate of *Crawford;*

b. emphasizes educational quality by improving the teaching of basics, keeping favorable student attitudes and enhancing teacher quality;

c. contains explicit plans for enhancing community acceptance and for avoiding family flight and provides for local parental participation in decision making;

d. is fair and stays fair;

e. explicitly deals with issues of safety; and

f. buses grades 4-9 most willingly, and if possible avoids busing pupils from kindergarten and from grades 1-3.

Issues of feasibility and cost lie outside the scope of this discussion.

This report was probably the most important output of the project. In thus displaying Board values explicitly, it apparently did serve as a guide to District planners. It foreshadows in considerable detail the characteristics of the plan ultimately adopted by the Board.

PLANS

While I was obtaining importance weights, various individuals and organizations were developing plans. At least some of those external groups involved in plan preparation were well-informed about the VAS and had access to Board weights prior to submission of their plans, and so presumably could have exploited this information in plan preparation. There is no evidence that this occurred.

Dr. Lawson and I made the decisions about which plans we would evaluate by means of VAS. All those rejected were, in our judgment, too vague for analysis—except for one metropolitan plan, which we rejected in part because it seemed politically and legally infeasible and in part because VAS was not well suited to its analysis.

VAS was eventually applied to eight plans:

BEST submitted a plan heavily emphasizing voluntarism and centers of excellence. Its voluntary characteristics made demographic analysis especially difficult.

BUSTOP also submitted a basically voluntary plan, though quite different in character from BEST's.

CACSI's plan was essentially the one rejected previously by the Board, though updated in various fairly minor ways. It was not voluntary.

COBA (the Council of Black Administrators), an advisory group composed primarily of Principals of LAUSD schools, submitted a nonvoluntary plan.

Dr. John Caughey, Professor Emeritus of History at UCLA, submitted a fairly thorough plan that had been prepared by a group consisting primarily of him and his students.

The Integration Project submitted a remarkable plan. By some estimates, it called for busing up to 80% of all students in the District. Its cost, highest of those submitted, was roughly seven times that of the least expensive plan.

We included Exhibit A, the plan originally submitted to Judge Egly and rejected by him. Although it had already been rejected by Judge Egly, we felt that it might serve as a baseline against which to evaluate other plans. It was a partially voluntary plan; its compulsory features were part-time; it included elaborate and sophisticated plans for enhancing community acceptance.

Finally, we analysed what we called Plan O, the state of the District in 1976-1977, in order to provide a basis for calculation of benefit/cost ratios.

The term 'plan' is misleading. Except for Exhibit A and Plan O (the former elaborately prepared by District staff and the latter a report of past events), no plan specified what should be done in detail. All plans were well-supplied with hortatory statements of principle—principles often hard to translate into detailed analysis of which pupils might attend which schools with what consequences. Some plans chose parts of the District for more detailed analysis, but left what would happen in the remainder of the District at the statement of principles level. Plans emphasizing voluntarism were especially hard to evaluate, since they could not, by their nature, spell out in detail what consequences of adoption might be.

None of this is surprising or unreasonable. Exhibit A, for example, is a massive, three-volume report (with a fourth volume of appendices). It had taken planners from the District staff more than six months and an enormous number of man-hours to prepare. No private group could be expected to have such resources —and Judge Egly's Minute Order specified a 90-day time limit on plan preparation.

Our final report to the Board stated that it was essential to understand the basis for staff judgments about the plans. Since plans were incompletely specified and often vague, staff members had little choice but to take at face value the statements in the plans, especially those concerned with subjective values. Feasibility and cost often could not be determined from plan documents. As a result, if a plan specifically called, for example, for maintenance of educational quality, with sufficient elaboration to emphasize the concern, the plan would be likely to get high marks for educational quality issues, even though it did not describe in detail how they were to be approached or dealt with.

SINGLE-DIMENSION UTILITIES

Dr. Lawson took primary charge of the very complex and demanding task of determining single-dimension utilities.

The first task (which I performed) was to define in a reasonably thorough way both what kinds of judgments were to be made and how they were to be made. I prepared a set of instructions about how to make such judgments. I also prepared, in collaboration with Dr. Lawson, a definition of each value dimension and a set of rules of judging it. Two examples follow:

BMB. Availability of special programs for educationally disadvantaged pupils.

By "special programs for educationally disadvantaged pupils" we mean such programs as Title I, SB 90. A plan may or may not effect the educational benefits of the availability of such programs.

A plan that leaves these benefits about as available as they are not scores 50. A plan that substantially increases them scores 100. A plan that substantially decreases them scores 0. On that scale, simply judge where each plan falls. Note that in making such judgments, you should consider only the educational benefits of these programs. Financial impacts are considered elsewhere in the evaluation process.

Necessary information: Five scores.

Auxiliary information: Whatever you can tell us about how each plan effects the availability of special programs for educationally disadvantaged pupils.

EA. Number of additional classrooms required.

This item refers, not to cost, which is handled elsewhere, but to delays, administrative difficulties, and the like. We would like a score based on needs for additional classrooms. Under Plan O, the following needs have been estimated.

Year	Needs under Plan 0	Score
1977-1978	185	88
1978-1979	150	90
1979-1980	205	83
1980-1981	253	84
1981-1982	190	88

Estimate the number of additional classrooms needed for each year under a plan. Then obtain a score as follows:

Score = 1 — [(1600 — number needed)/1600)].

Necessary information: Five scores.

Auxiliary information: Your basis for judgment.

It took at least a paragraph to describe each twig; some took several pages. At lower levels of the tree, the information was often repetitious. We modified the details for some of these scoring instructions as a result of feedback from those attempting to make the required calculations or judgments.

Dr. Lawson identified a set of staff analysis teams composed of LAUSD staff. The intent, not always fulfilled, was to have a team of at least five people expert on each significant subject-matter area included within the value tree. Some teams made judgments about just one twig; others were responsible for a number of them, all calling for the same kind of expertise. Each team leader was responsible for coordinating the efforts of the members of his or her team, and for ensuring that the resulting consensus judgment would represent team opinion and would also respond correctly to the instructions. There were 42 different teams, including a total of almost 70 LAUSD employees in varying combinations. Most had to work under extraordinary time pressure. Nevertheless, (with perhaps a few exceptions) each team member read all plans and made considered judgments about them—

sometimes as individuals and sometimes in team meetings. Teams often communicated with plan originators about the meaning of their plans.

This effort began with a meeting of all team members, in which Dr. Lawson and I explained the VAS, distributed instructions, and remained to answer all questions about their meaning. After that, the teams worked apart from us—except for frequent phone calls. Some of these calls simply requested clarification of instructions, others pointed out errors or misconceptions that led us to revise the instructions.

As filled-in single-dimension utilities response sheets came in, a small staff team headed by Dr. Lawson reviewed each for conformity to instructions, and, in a few cases, reasonableness. Two associate superintendents also reviewed these sheets. The reviewing was done under great time pressure. It caught a number of errors of interpretation. In every case, the appropriate staff analysis team, not Dr. Lawson, prepared the revised judgments. Often, a query from a reviewer to a staff analysis team simply produced a reaffirmation of the original numbers along with a more detailed rationale for them. We accepted all such reaffirmations. In my opinion, staff judgments of single-dimension utilities were sophisticated and unbiased. If any bias existed, it probably was in favor of Exhibit A, simply because it was so much more detailed and therefore so much easier to work with than other plans.

Demographic projections, needed primarily in Branch A, were a special problem. No such projections were available, or could be made available, at the levels of detail required by VAS. All we had was a school-by-school racial-ethnic breakdown for 1976-1977, a District-wide grade-by-grade breakdown for the same year, and some District-wide forecasts of racial-ethnic populations as a function of year. We used these numbers (and several sophisticated computer programs, some prepared by Dr. Frank Toggenburger of LAUSD and some by Richard John, a graduate student of mine at USC), to extrapolate to school-by-school effects of various plans as best we could. Such extrapolations could not, of course, take into account pupil population changes that might, or might not, follow actual implementation of the plan, and were unsatisfactory in various other ways. Our final report to the Board said:

> Because of time pressures and missing data, many approximations went into these calculations and judgments. Of particular importance is that we have school-by-school racial-ethnic breakdowns only for 1976-77. Consequently, all calculation having to do with demographic issues were based on these data.

This statement was too simple, since we also used the grade-by-grade breakdown and the racial-ethnic forecasts in these calculations.

RESULTS

Table 7 presents benefit/cost ratios (for Board weights; the ratios for other weighters are similar), overall benefits, and overall costs for each plan, each source of weights, and each of the two years analysed.[1]

BUSTOP did not supply information needed for cost calculations. We calculated benefit/cost ratios only if they were positive—that is, if the benefit of the plan being considered was greater than that of Plan O. This often did not occur.

Exhibit A was the clear winner, on benefit/cost ratio, and for all but one weighter on benefits. The ordering of plans differed little among weighters, primarily for technical reasons discussed below. Dr. Sullivan's benefit measures were below those of other weighters in almost all cases primarily because he assigned a considerably higher weight to Branch D, Implications for District Personnel, than did the other weighters. Most plans fared relatively poorly on Branch D, for all weighters.

Table 8 presents the scores for each plan on the six major values at the top of the value tree, using Board weights only. While the plans vary substantially from one dimension to another, their major features are highly visible. For example, the CACSI and Integration Project plans do very well on Racial-Ethnic Compo-

Table 7: Summary of Benefits and Costs

	BEST	BUSTOP	CACSI	CAUGHEY	COBA	Int. P.	Exh. A.	Plan 0
YEAR: 1978-1979								
Benefit/Cost Ratio								
5 Board members	.071	–	.027	–	.035	.005	.222	–
Overall Benefit								
5 Board members	57	50	66	49	54	56	68	53
BEST	55	55	63	50	51	58	70	52
Dr. Havighurst	52	48	64	53	52	58	63	51
Dr. Miller	56	52	63	43	62	51	70	52
Dr. Sullivan	50	46	56	43	47	50	64	52
Annual incremental operating cost (noncumulative)	37.2	NA	69.4	50.9	41.1	122.1	52.7	–
+ Incremental capital costs (cumulative)	18.8	NA	412.5	327.1	163.5	496.3	14.8	–
= Cumulative incremental cost	56.0	NA	481.9	378.0	204.5	618.4	67.5	–

45

Table 7 (Continued)

	BEST	BUSTOP	CACSI	CAUGHEY	COBA	Int. P.	Exh. A.	Plan 0
YEAR: 1981-1982								
Benefit/Cost Ratio								
5 Board members	.039	–	.026	–	.014	.007	.177	–
Overall Benefit								
5 Board members	60	51	69	52	62	58	71	53
BEST	63	54	68	50	56	59	74	52
Dr. Havighurst	58	48	69	57	60	59	67	51
Dr. Miller	62	53	68	45	66	51	74	52
Dr. Sullivan	50	49	60	46	55	50	69	52
Annual incremental operating cost (noncumulative)	95.1	NA	94.9	92.0	143.7	151.6	73.0	–
+ Incremental capital costs (cumulative)	83.3	NA	516.4	520.2	517.0	549.2	28.9	–
= Cumulative incremental cost	180.4	NA	611.3	612.2	660.7	700.8	101.9	–

46

Table 8: Value Profile for Each Plan Using Board Weights

5 Board Members	BEST	BUSTOP	CACSI	CAUGHEY	COBA	Int. P.	Exh. A.	Plan 0
YEAR: 1978-1979								
A. R-E Compositions	46	43	73	71	51	83	50	28
B. Educational Quality	57	57	72	47	54	53	77	54
C. Community Acceptance	66	43	57	34	56	52	69	55
D. Effects on District Personnel	34	42	36	35	29	28	48	66
E. Destabilizing Effects	69	55	80	63	66	58	73	72
F. Monitoring and Evaluation	50	50	50	50	66	45	71	50
YEAR: 1981-1982								
A. R-E Compositions	60	43	70	77	79	84	51	28
B. Educational Quality	62	57	80	48	59	54	81	54
C. Community Acceptance	68	43	54	35	57	55	70	55
D. Effects on District Personnel	24	51	50	46	39	36	57	66
E. Destabilizing Effects	68	55	82	70	74	57	82	72
F. Monitoring and Evaluation	50	50	50	50	66	41	61	50

sitions, the CACSI plan does well on Destabilizing Effects, while Exhibit A does well on Educational Quality, Community Acceptance, and Destabilizing Effects. It surprised us that the two voluntary plans (BEST and BUSTOP) did not do better on Educational Quality than they did. Perhaps this is because their necessarily incomplete and vague nature left staff analysis teams with relatively little basis for judging how their strong declarations in favor of educational quality were to be put into practice.

A great deal more information than that contained in Tables 4 and 5 was presented to the Board in our final report. But these two tables capture the highlights.

AFTERMATH

The Board and Judge Egly accepted the volume resulting from this work as an elaborate and thorough response to the requirements of the Minute Order concerning analyses of external plans.

But an obvious and major omission from the analysis was the plan that the Board finally adopted. Time pressure made inclusion of that plan in the original work of the staff analysis teams impossible. The Board's plan evolved very rapidly, in a period of one week, from a series of fragmentary parts of plans that had been prepared and considered earlier. Wording changes were still in progress up to the very last moment prior to printing deadlines. In no way could the unwieldy staff analysis teams have completed their analytic and judgmental tasks in time to permit use of VAS.

When the deadline set by Judge Egly arrived, he was on vacation. We could have used the VAS to evaluate the Board plan during the vacation period, after its submission. This idea was considered, but rejected by those responsible for such decisions. No explanation was given to me of the basis for that rejection. A natural basis was that the plan had already been adopted by the Board and submitted to the judge. Collection of the judgments entering into VAS was a costly and demanding process. Moreover, issues of unreliability and bias might have been raised since the Board's plan would have been considered at a time and under circumstances different from all others.

In spite of various legal challenges, Judge Egly ordered that the Board's new plan be implemented as a first step toward desegregating the District. During the course of that implementation process, it has inevitably undergone numerous changes, responsive to the changing characteristics of the problem, to various forms of public response, and perhaps to a changing judicial recognition of the severity of the problems that must still be solved if LAUSD is to desegregate effectively.

On September 12, 1978, the Los Angeles School Board began execution of the desegregation plan it had adopted, as modified during the previous spring and summer. On October 23, 1978, the District announced the results of its latest racial survey of pupils. Total number of pupils was 555,755. Other White enrollment was 29.8%. There was 38.5% Hispanic-American pupils, 24.7% Blacks, and 7% Asian-American and other minorities.

While some decrease of enrollment had been expected (the District had been dropping about 2% per year for the last 8 years or so), the 15% decrease this year is startling, as is the 3.8% decrease in the percentage of Other Whites among pupils as a whole. Various statistics, including especially details of enrollment in grades subject to forced busing and substantial losses in schools in the mostly White San Fernando Valley, suggest that this plan, like others elsewhere, is leading to substantial amounts of "white flight"—loss of White pupils from the District as a result of forced desegregation. The unexpected loss of 15% of enrollment, compared with last year's 2.9%, suggests that perhaps pupils from other racial-ethnic groups are fleeing the District as well.

In Los Angeles, what does school desegregation mean? How can it be achieved?

TECHNICAL ISSUES

Complexity

The value tree is, of course, preposterously complex from a strictly technical point of view. It concerns itself with 144 measures.' From a technical point of view, 8 would be about right and 15 would already be excessive.

I have argued the reasons why such complexity was necessary and inevitable above. Aside from requiring enormously increased effort, the complexity blunted the meaningfulness of the weights. No weighter assigned any high-level value a weight of 0. But in the absence of zero weights, the net result was an extremely complex averaging process, in which judgments about individual values were counterbalanced by judgments about other individual values. The result was that, although differences among weighters appear throughout the value tree, they have relatively little influence in the highly aggregated numbers that represent plan benefits.

The point can be overemphasized. Studies of multiattribute utility measurement routinely find that such procedures turn what seems like major disagreement into a relatively high degree of agreement (see, for example, Gardiner and Edwards, 1975; Aschenbrenner, 1976). That clearly happened in this case also. The Board members would have been surprised, as I was, to see how small the standard deviations of their normalized weights for higher-level values were. (If the two nonparticipating members had chosen to participate, they probably would not have increased those standard deviations to any substantial degree.) In fact, it was fortunate that Dr. Sullivan was one of the weighters. His weights differed markedly from those of others in many ways. This led to a change in overall benefit for all plans for him, but to little change in rank ordering.

Of course the structural complexity of the value tree invites alternative organizations. It is surprising and pleasant that only one such suggestion was made; it was regarded as inappropriate by all those who considered it other than the organization that made it.

The ability of all respondents to work with such complex judgments in such a complex structure seemed remarkable to me. I doubt that they could have done so had they not all been experts on education and integration. Even so, the amount of time and effort each weighter put into his or her weights was surprising and impressive.

Assumptions and Procedures

Any decision analyst will recognize the wealth of simplifying assumptions that entered into this analysis. They include: use of a linear model for aggregation, use of linear or triangular utility functions instead of functions more directly elicited, and use of averages as a way of aggregating judgments over people. While such assumptions have major technical significance, I do not see how this sort of analysis could have been done without them. And I am skeptical that any other multiattribute utility measurement procedure, if it could have somehow been carried out, would have led to different orderings of the plans.

The ratio judgments procedure used in collecting weights was, as it turns out, unnecessarily complex. Enormous simplifications are possible, based on the fact that a rank ordering of values already contains a great deal of metric information. A paper describing these simplifications is in preparation.

Procedures for eliciting single-dimension utility functions seemed to work relatively well. While members of staff analysis teams sometimes differed, they usually had little difficulty in reconciling those differences—once all understood the instructions clearly.

The most important procedural message of this study concerns the importance of involving all stakeholders in any evaluative process. While the basic structure of the value tree remained unchanged, failure to consult all stakeholders would have led to omission of several of significant dimensions of value. Moreover, many of the stakeholders developed, in the course of our frequent meetings with them, an interest in and understanding of the process that otherwise could never have been obtained.

CONCLUSION

I was disappointed that the Board's final plan was not analyzed by VAS. A possible conclusion is that formal analysis, such as VAS provided, is not an acceptable substitute for political processes.

In spite of its technical shortcomings reviewed above, I was satisfied with the analytic process, and believed its conclusions. In particular, the superiority of Exhibit A and CACSI to the other plans was, in my opinion, very real. In part, it reflected the relative amounts of professional expertise of the planners in working with an extremely complex school system, and in part it reflected the greater length of time available to the preparers of those plans. (CACSI, of course, prepared the plan in all essentials long before Judge Egly issued the Minute Order that specified a 90-day deadline for submission of all plans.)

My other primary conclusion concerns the quality of my collaborators. The efforts of Dr. Lawson and Mr. McMullen were brilliant. The contributions of other LAUSD staff members were of major importance; there were too many of them, and their contributions were too diverse, to acknowledge individually here. But my admiration for the ability and dedication of those with whom I worked is unqualified.

Would I recommend these procedures, or some modification of them, for evaluating plans in other major social contexts? Yes. In fact, I have done so (Edwards, 1972, 1978).

Major problems concerning the relation between the problem and the methods remain unsolved. Most important is that of reducing the number of dimensions of evaluation. Of secondary but still substantial importance is the elicitation process for single-dimension utility functions, particularly as it relates to what position is assigned to the status quo.

But I would never advise that anyone attempt so complex an analysis in two months! And, before participating in another such effort, I would want a clearer specification of the roles of analytic vis-a-vis political processes in reaching a final decision. Finally, it was frustrating to work with inadequate demographic data. If an analysis of an issue as demographically complex as desegregation is needed, it should be preceded by preparation of a far more elaborate set of demographic projections.

SUMMARY

An elaborate multiattribute utility analysis was made of seven school desegregation plans submitted by external groups to the Los Angeles School Board, which was under court order to desegregate. District officials, board members, plaintiffs, and intervenors in the court case provided evaluative dimensions. Weights for these dimensions were elicited from the above, plus several professional experts. District staff made judgments of the probable performance of each plan on each evaluative dimension. Aggregate measures of benefits and of benefit/cost ratios were computed. The only plan not so evaluated was the one which the Board ultimately adopted.

NOTE

1. Time pressures and complexity combined to force us to use a computer program to do the calculations, though we had originally planned to do them by hand. I am grateful to John Hoelzl, William Gabrielli, and William Stillwell, all of SSRI, for their late hours and last-minute success.

REFERENCES

ASCHENBRENNER, K. M. (1976) "Multiattribute Bewertung Medizinischer Therapiealternatives." Research Report, SFB 24, Univ. of Mannheim.

DAWES, R. M. and B. CORRIGAN (1974) "Linear models in decision making." Psychological Bulletin 81, 2: 95-106.

EDWARDS, W. (1972) "Social utilities," in Decision and Risk Analysis: Powerful New Tools for Management. Proceedings of the Sixth Triennial Symposium, June 1971, Hoboken. Engineering Economist, pp. 119-129.

——— (1972) "How to use multiattribute utility measurement for social decision making." IEEE Transactions on Systems, Man and Cybernetics 7: 326-340.

——— and von WINTERFELDT, D. (1973a) "Costs and payoffs in perceptual research." Engineering Psychology Laboratory Report (Univ. of Michigan) #011313-1-T, October.

——— (1973b) "Evaluation of complex stimuli using multiattribute utility procedures." Engineering Psychology Laboratory Report (Univ. of Michigan) #011313-2-T, October.

——— (1973c) "Flat maxima in linear optimization models." Engineering Psychology Report (Univ. of Michigan) #011313-4-T, November.

GARDINER, P. C. and W. EDWARDS (1975) "Public values: multiattribute utility measurement for social decision making," in M. F. Kaplan and S. Schwartz (eds.) Human Judgment and Decision Processes. New York: Academic Press.

KEENEY, R. L. and H. RAIFFA (1976) Decisions with Multiple Objectives: Preferences and Value Tradeoffs. New York: John Wiley.

YNTEMA, D. B. and W. S. TORGERSON (1961) "Man-computer cooperation in decisions requiring common sense." IRE. Transactions of the Professional Group on Human Factors in Electronics. HFE 2, 1: 20-26.

Robert E. Stake
University of Illinois at Urbana-Champaign

2

VALIDATING REPRESENTATIONS
The Evaluator's Responsibility

Persons having the responsibility to evaluate some program are expected to pass judgment on its worth. At the moment of evaluation, their responsibility is not primarily responsibility to understand, nor a responsibility to discern the causes of some effect, nor to make a decision about that program. The evaluation responsibility is a responsibility to make judgments.

Sometimes the people who have the real responsibility for evaluating delegate or contract to have an evaluation study done. Often they call in evaluation specialists. These specialists who do evaluation studies are not evaluators, theirs is not a responsibility to evaluate but to assist the people who do have the responsibility to evaluate.

Evaluation specialists are expected to facilitate. Their primary responsibility is not to render judgments, nor to find causes, nor to recommend action. Those might be activities their sponsors want, and the contract may call for them, but they are not implicit in the responsibility of the evaluation specialist. What is critical is that the evaluation specialist is to provide assistance to people, the constituents, who have the responsibility to make value-judgments.

When I say "constituents," I am thinking of such people as school administrators, funding agents, public relations agents, lobbyists, taxpapers, students, teachers, and similar people in social program areas other than education. Each of these constituent groups, each of the persons within the groups, has the responsibility to evaluate.

Each also has a share in the power to influence the enterprise, particularly in the power to hurt it. There is a distribution of power, seldom manifested clearly as hands upon the tiller, but however abstract and diffuse, there is a distribution of power.

* * *

Allow me to claim at the outset of this chapter that the ethics of the evaluation specialist should be such that the mere act of carrying out an evaluation study should not in itself result in a change in the power structure. The degree of control over social programs should not be altered—according to this ethical precept —for any constituent member merely because an evaluation study has occurred.

I am not going on to say that the *findings* should be interpreted or acted upon in the way that will leave the power structure unchanged. I am not talking about the study's findings at all. I am talking about the condition of having an evaluation study—that condition alone should not cause a change in power, and the evaluation specialist should be pledged to restraining any change in power that might occur merely because an evaluation study is being carried out.

Of course it is impossible to keep the power structure completely unchanged. Persons holding new information, whether the information is accurate or relevant, increase their control over the program (MacDonald, 1974; Cohen, 1973).

It used to be said that "knowledge is power." It is now more apparent that "information is power." Even the appearance of being informed is correlated with power.

For the evaluation specialist to have no influence on the power configuration is impossible, but the ethical responsibility of the evaluation specialist is to minimize the advantage persons gain (or lose) merely because an evaluation study occurs.

Let me acknowledge further that the evaluation specialist is a person with other roles to play in life. In their other roles they may work to improve the program or to change the power structure. The fact that they are evaluation specialists should not deny them the exercise of indignation nor the opportunity to protect a precious object in jeopardy. In their other roles they should make value judgments about the program, but not as specialists in evaluation. (For a contrary position see Scriven, 1967).

This too is impossible. No matter how well trained, people cannot separate their responsibilities to be dispassionate witnesses and facilitators from their responsibilities to advocate and reform. But the ethical code should call upon evaluation specialists to so strive.

They should also realize that they are taking unethical advantage of their stations when they try to improve the control or decision-making processes as part of their effort to assist in evaluation.

I believe that most evaluation specialists would subscribe to the ethical principle of leaving the power structure unchanged, but object to my claim that it is unethical to help improve the decision-making function, especially to make it more explicit and less intuitive, if accomplished under the guise of an evaluation service. Most of my colleagues enter into the evaluation study with an unabashed enthusiasm to help clean up the control of the program.

In this chapter I contend that in so doing they contribute in a small way to the technologizing and disintegration of our society.

Perhaps it is a small flaw in the social fabric. But it is our flaw, and our ethical standards should help us mend it.

* * *

The state of evaluation services as a whole reveals a much larger flaw in the social fabric. Program evaluation is in an unhealthy condition. It is extremely costly. It is not facilitating very well, other than to provide an image that the *sponsors* are acting responsibly, are becoming informed, and are moving toward the alleviation of the problems they were commissioned to work on.

Here and around the world there is a massive investment in formal evaluation mechanisms, throughout government and other institutions and agencies. The cost of evaluation is enormous. Clark Abt (1976) has recently summarized the scope of activities. The cost of evaluation is enormous.

The public that ultimately foots the bill, and even the evaluation sponsors, seldom get their money's worth, at least not in terms of the information generated. That information often contributes to the knowing-better-than-before the values of the program, but it is an extremely costly purchase.

The cost of the evaluation of Project Follow-Through has run over $30 million—and we know only a small bit more about the education of Headstart children as they move on into the primary grades of public school.

Evaluation costs in the Experimental Schools program ran up to a quarter of a million dollars in each of the participating school districts, but we learned very little about what schools can accomplish if they are relieved of budget constraints.

Other evaluation studies are much less expensive, yet consistently their authors tell us that the phenomena examined require more elaborate designs and greater investments. Research proposals promise a readiness to do the job that is belied by the final reports.

It can be argued that these costs are costs that we can afford. In addition to the information gained there are other benefits from evaluation studies. One is the contribution we continue to make to an ethic of public accountability. Another is the contribution to a healthy skepticism about the innovations of the day.

There are other costs than money costs, of course. There are costs to the political system, to which I referred earlier.

Part of the cost of evaluation studies is the subtle and irrational redistribution of power in public affairs. More power devolves to those who hold the information, to those who commission the studies, to those (family social scientists) who legitimate research designs and representations—and away from those who are supposed to be the beneficiaries of the social programming.

Support for this view of the effects of evaluation is found in the writings of many who study contemporary social affairs, in the writing, for example, of Gideon Sjoberg (1975), Ernest House

(1973), and in the fine review of the first *Handbook* by Lee Cronbach's Stanford Evaluation Consortium (see Ross and Cronbach, 1976).

Few of us with this view are suggesting that the acquisition of power is usually a direct and conscious aim of evaluation specialists or their patrons. Their common aim is improve the delivery of social services. But the result is a redefinition of the social service and a more controlling position for certain parties.

In 1977 Don Campbell wrote, "We evaluation methodologists are in fact developing alternative political systems." It is unreasonable to suppose that these new systems would have the same balance, or imbalance of power as before.

A most insightful statement was made recently about "Evaluation and the Quest for Control of Public Programs" for participants of PASITAM, Program of Advanced Studies in Institution Building and Technical Assistance Methodology. In the Summer 1978 PASITAM Newsletter Russell Stout wrote:

> The preoccupation with evaluation is inspired by the yearning for "control." We want to prove that we can set targets, plan to meet them, and realize the plan. . . .
>
> There is a lot of innocence in the assumption that we can sensibly control bureaucratic agencies through formal processes. . . . why kid ourselves with formal evaluation processes? Why not acknowledge that controlling public organizations is a political, not a technical issue. Then we can more rationally criticize agencies and programs on the basis of "preference," not just formal measures of apparent efficiency and effectiveness. . . .
>
> An excessive preoccupation with program evaluation and formal control spurs the bureaucratization of politics and the professionalization of public policy, making genuinely political choices seem more and more apolitical. Yet shifting political issues into the domain of experts does not change their inherent nature.
>
> The trouble with expert politics is that it reduces our ability to start or abandon programs on the basis of *preference*. It puts the overt focus on the *means* at the expense of open attention to the ends.

The expert evaluator makes assumptions about means-ends relationships and often participates in the hidden political process of program development and implementation. Then the question of what is desirable (including what is possible) is recast in this form: How might a possibility be realized? And assumptions and issues about means pre-empt concerns with ends.

As methods of implementation, and concurrently, methods of evaluation, crowd into attention, other concerns, particularly the original concerns of the program constituents, are nudged aside. This may or may not be bad. People should be free to change attentions, to concentrate less on goals and more on means, if they choose. It is bad only if this change occurs automatically, as if it were necessary to focus on implementation and monitoring and less on the problems themselves. It is bad if it interferes with immediate efforts to alleviate—under the presumption that it is important first to work out technically sound methods of alleviation.

* * *

The meetings of the Florida Educational Research Association had just ended. Jack, Bernadine, and I sat in the warm sun, trying to think of an image or metaphor. We weren't having much luck.

What I wanted was something to cause instant recognition of what some people do—directors, bureaucrats, researchers, it doesn't make any difference—the ones who are forever reorganizing their places, drawing up a new general plan. Was "dervish" what I had in mind? No that wasn't it.

I was really rather put out. Jack had persuaded me that in my paper I had used the term dilettante wrong as if it meant over-specialized rather than amateurish. And I was bothered by yesterday's presentations of elaborate matrices for district record keeping of student achievement. My mind seemed to be on too many tracks.

I wanted a word that pointed out that that person was able to actually avoid responsibility by getting people fixated on details, such as the organization chart or task-analysis results.

The education people in Florida were apparently under a lot of pressure to think about curriculum and instruction in terms of specific objectives. Those at every school found it necessary to make statements of what they were trying to teach and what student learnings should be tested. I had heard a couple of presentations about how the whole thing could be set up and monitored with computer-stored matrices. That is, if you list all the students down this side and put all the basic objectives across this edge, you can just check off what has been done and see what remains to be done.

Jack brought me back, suggesting perhaps I was talking about a "butter and eggs man." Apparently that term had become popular in maybe the thirties to represent the guy who has his finger in every pie. Well, I rather liked the term; but it didn't do it. I wanted it to indicate clearly that the people were not getting the butter and eggs or whatever it was they needed.

Bernadine thought maybe I was thinking of a flimflam man. But no, these people were not playing the confidence game; they were people who really believed that they were doing the right thing by rearranging their organizations and planning new programs. At least some of them. I wondered if there had not been some such character in "How to Succeed in Business Without Really Trying." Jack said that there was that guy who arranged for the board members to watch the girl in the bikini while he was giving his budget report. But I was thinking more of a puffer-fish than a shark. It just wasn't my day.

It seemed so terrible to me to be representing the education of all the children in Florida in terms of a couple hundred objectives. Of course, I know that many educators and parents want a clear-cut approach—and that one can argue that you have to do the basics first if you want to get anywhere with the finer things. But it seemed so obvious that you could perpetually deny children the opportunities of learning the finer things this way, that you gave them ugly models of learners and learning, that you were saying that it wasn't important whether or not their life was intellectually enriched those hundreds of hours they spent in a school room.

These people were really trying to do their job. They had promises to live up to. And before they could carry out those promises they had to get ready to carry out the promises.

The school official can expect to be in office for perhaps only three years. Then he will move on to another office or to another place. Each time he moves into a new responsibility he sees that the problems are great, that his predecessor had arranged things in a peculiar way, and that some of those problems just can't be overlooked. So he sets up a new organization. Or a new plan of action. New promises, new promises in the form of charts of objectives, organization charts.

People yearn for something better from their officials. They want to believe that this time they are going to get their money's worth. They don't want a Don Quixote, tilting imaginary windmills and dreaming impossible dreams. But what about the dream, the impossible dream, that the next reorganization will get more done than the last?

And the smart director or researcher or bureaucrat, whether conscious of it or not, uses that dream to protect himself, calling for others to draw up specific plans, showing long lists of expectations, rationalizing the problems. . . .

But I just couldn't think of the metaphor for it.

*   *   *

One grand obstacle to the alleviation of social distress is the belief that *rationalism* is a sound conceptual orientation for problem solving. It is supposed that well-reasoned models, that careful specification of dependent elements, that optimized service-delivery calculations, will increase the chance of remediation.

It is a magnificent presumption that social problems will yield to rational thinking, that faults in our educational system will be best attacked by planning, research, and monitoring. We found the presumption widespread in a recent interactive field study (Stake and Easley, 1978) of science teaching for the National Science Foundation: that administrative competence was seen to be formalistic: identifying the links between action and intent, identifying the indicator variables that reveal the success of an action, and maximizing the effort to improve scores on those indicator variables.

Long-experienced school administrators know that the process of education at best poorly fits such rational models. "Productivity" and "bottom line" are common images, but poor representations of the diffuse and organic outcomes of education. Results of schooling are not well indicated by tests of competence or by attitude-rating scales, not because the test development is inadequate, but because the conceptualizatin is inadequate.

The disconnection between action and intent in education is most apparent in local obstacles to teaching, idiosyncracies usually not specified in a rational model and usually not recognizable in the regression of student performance on aptitude and effort. Remedy lies in working directly with those localized disconnections, the obstacles of the individual situation—but the presumption abides. Instead of treating the task of education as a uniqueness among its people, its experience, its situation, we find the work of the school being simplified and targeted, made more uniform across situations. Many present practices of evaluation specialists contribute to this questionable rationalism.

The error of the evaluation specialists, I think, is not primarily one of too much interest in the universals of human behavior, nor the imperfections in their experimental or statistical controls. It is not that a technological approach cannot assist in the evaluation of social programs. The outstanding error, I believe, is one of inadequate representations of field situations, that is measurement error, but a qualitative rather than a quantitative misrepresentation.

The problem has been not so much an overcommitment to technology, but a failure to question adequately the technology we use. We have tended to trust an elegant simplification, especially when it brought statistical significance. Our willingness to tolerate *gross* approximations to the social situation has been at fault. As Robert Macnamara did in Vietnam (Halberstam, 1972) we believe in indicators that fail to indicate.

* * *

As claimed in the opening sentences of this chapter, the evaluation specialist's responsibility is primarily one of assisting constituents to make judgments about the quality of the program. To repeat, it is not one of finding causes of certain effects, nor of passing judgment as an independent observer, nor of recommending action. The primary responsibility is helping all those who have the existing and continuing responsibility for control prepare themselves to make new judgments.

The evaluation specialist is to assist those who will judge. How can assistance best be provided? How can it be provided without diminishing certain value positions, certain preferences, certain social or political groups?

I think that it can best be provided by careful attention to constituents: to their conceptualizations, issues, value positions, and experience. This means that usually instead of drawing from the conceptualizations of the social sciences and its research methodologies, the evaluation specialist should build upon the realities perceived by those people.

As evaluation specialists we should not purport to teach people to think in new terms, with new constructs, with new valuation of evidence—though of course we may introduce previously unrealized happenings, and people may end up thinking new thoughts. We should not say, "you need to see this as a researcher sees it." Readers should have the opportunity to work their way into more abstract or theoretical writings, such as in the literature of the disciplines, but the basic description of what is happening should be in language readers have already mastered.

For example, evaluation specialists should be extremely hesitant to use the Flanders Interaction Analysis checklist in the classroom because it transforms the description of teacher-student interactions into abstractions, unfamiliar to most evaluation study audiences. The same goes for most instruments and techniques, both old and new.

It becomes easy to presume that what has *not* been represented has been found not to be important.

But it is not enough to limit ourselves to language and issues of the people in and around the program. Techniques such as the prioritization of goals or projections of utility of alternate plan take ordinary words, the ideas of constituents, and combine and transform them into representations of iceberg proportions, partly seen, largely unseen.

In chapter 1 we were introduced to Ward Edwards's value tree. It is a complex representation of complex utilities for social problems of staggering complexity. Perhaps, then, no representation can be valid. The utility of something is of course only partially realized in the real world. The representation of the utility in the tree is visible, yet obscure, sensitive to the assumptions and constraints of the model, most of which are not apparent to the constituent parties.

Ward's data collection apparently involves careful explanation but this does not assure that the resulting tree is understandable. He noted the many complexities. Those readers most audacious will use the iceberg to further their aims. Those readers most literal and subdued will presume that others see evidence that they cannot.

I would not censure Ward Edwards for creating his tree. Like Joyce Kilmer I admire the creators of trees. I admire the internal integrity of his representation. I would be greatly dismayed if our measurements technology failed to devise elegant representations of the phenomena of education.

But I am aghast at the quickness with which my evaluation colleagues insert new and untested devices into their fieldwork plan. Ward Edwards might be subject to censure here. What evidence has he that the Los Angeles situation was not misrepresented by the value tree?

All of us in this business as professionals have a pressing obligation to provide valid representations. Our emphases recently on validation studies have been woefully weak. Evaluation specialists are blase about the quality of their representations.

To be valid these representations should resist the internal and external threats posed by Campbell and Stanley (1963); but in the direction pointed by Cronbach (1971) they should be consonant with their expected uses. Our representations should be meaningful, comprehensible to more sophisticated and less sophisticated audiences as well. Understanding them should not depend on some still-to-be-developed audience readiness, they should be tailored to existing audience readinesses.

Most of my colleagues in evaluation methodology will say I ask too much. How could they abandon the concept maps, the instruments, the analytic techniques, they have come to find powerful? They say it is the audiences who should educate themselves. That may work for graduate school but not when the audiences include the constituents of public service programs.

To respond to the assistance responsibility it appears we must abandon a number of principles of traditional social science research. At the second CTB/McGraw Hill National Conference on Testing (San Francisco, September 21-22, 1978) both Lee Cronbach and Michael Scriven spoke to this issue. Some attractive alternatives appear in the direction of naturalistic inquiry (Guba, 1978; Stake, 1978).

At the turn of the century, German philosopher Wilhelm Dilthey (1910) claimed that more objective and "scientific" studies did not do the best job of acquainting man with himself.

> Only from his actions, his fixed utterances, his effects upon others, can man learn about himself; thus he learns to know himself only by the round-about way of understanding. What we once were, how we developed and became what we are, we learn from the way in which we acted, the plans which we once adopted, the way in which we made ourselves felt in our vocation, from old dead letters, from judgments on which were spoken long ago . . . we understand ourselves and others only when we transfer our own lived experience into every kind of expression of our own and other people's lives.

He distinguished between the human studies and other kinds of studies.

> The human studies are thus founded on this relation between lived experience, expression, and understanding. Here for the first time we reach a clear criterion by which the delimitation of the human studies can be definitively carried out. A study belongs to the human studies only if its object becomes accessible to use

through the attitude which is founded on the relation between life, expression, and understanding.

Dilthey was not urging us merely to pay more attention to humanistic values or to put more affective variables into our equations. He was saying that our methods of studying human affairs need to capitalize upon the natural powers of people to experience and understand.

A more naturalistic, experiential approach to evaluation studies is now finding support here and there across America, Australia, and northern Europe. Ethnographic observations are moving from the periphery of some designs to the center. Case studies are seen, more and more, as an important research tool for extending experience and understanding.

As Dilthey emphasized, intentionality and empathy are central to the comprehension of social problem. So also is information holistic and episodic. Such comprehension continues to be disdained by many researchers as inherently subjective, and therefore biased (Page, in press) and a poor basis for generalization, but disappointments with more rationalistic efforts to create generalizations has swung support to naturalistic studies (Guba, 1978; Smith, in press). Ward Edwards's description earlier of his assistance to the Los Angeles Unified School District reminds us that good quantitative technologists can be good naturalistic reporters too.

While increased use of case studies may increase the relevance and comprehensibility of evaluation reports they of course offer no guarantee of representational validity. The naturalistic researcher too is tempted to concentrate on internal integrity of portrayals and to overlook misrepresentations. The vignette, for example, is a troublesome datum—it drives the message home but is it a trustworthy representation?

In our NSF study of science teaching we encountered great problems in assimilating findings from across the eleven sites. We were confortable with the composite representation, not deligted by it, and we had little to offer as evidence of validity.

Across twenty years of experience we program evaluators have come to realize we have placed too much emphasis on operationalization, covariance controls, sampling theory, and attitude scaling. We are only beginning to realize our overdependence on unvalidated representations.

* * *

I opened this chapter claiming it should be ethically improper for evaluation specialists to allow the mere fact of evaluation study to alter the power and control structures for social programs. Not only is such a standard proper, as I see it, but if seriously considered, it would help us realize our responsibility to assure meaningfulness in representations to our sponsors and other diverse constituents of the programs.

REFERENCES

ABT, C. (1976) "Supply, demands, motives and constraints of the evaluation producing community." Presented at the annual meeting of AERA. San Francisco, April.

CAMPBELL, D. T. (1977) "Keeping the data honest in the experimenting society," in H. W. Melton and D.J.H. Watson (eds.) Interdisciplinary Dimension of Accounting for Social Goals and Social Organizations. Columbus. OH: Grid.

——— and J. C. STANLEY (1963) "Experimental and quasi-experimental designs for research," pp. 171-246 in N. L. Gage (ed.) Handbook of Research on Teaching. Chicago: Rand McNally.

COHEN, D. K. (1973) "Politics and research," in E. House (ed.) School Evaluation: The Politics and Process. Berkeley: McCutchan.

CRONBACH, L. J. (1971) "Test validation," in R. L. Thorndike (ed.) Educational Measurement. Washington, DC: American Council on Education.

DILTHEY, W. (1910, 1914-1927) The Construction of the Historical World of the Human Studies. Gesammelte Schriften I-VII. Leipzig: B. G. Tuebner.

EDWARDS, W., M. GUTTENTAG, and K. SNAPPER (1975) "A decision-theoretic approach to evaluation research," pp. 139-181 in E. L. Struening and M. Guttentag (eds.) Handbook of Evaluation Research, Volume 1. Beverly Hills: Sage Publications.

GUBA, E. G. (1978) Toward a Methodology of Naturalistic Inquiry in Educational Evaluation. CSE Monograph No. 8. Los Angeles: Center for the Study of Evaluation, UCLA.

HALBERSTAM, D. (1972) The Best and the Brightest. New York: Random House.

HOUSE, E. R. [ed] (1973) School Evaluation: The Politics and Process. Berkeley: McCutchan.

MacDONALD, B. (1974) "Evaluation and the control of education," in his SAFARI: Innovation, Evaluation, Research and the Problem of Control. Norwich, England: Centre for Applied Research in Education, University of East Anglia.

PAGE, E. B. (in press) "Should educational evaluation be more objective or more subjective? more objective." Journal of Evaluation and Policy Studies in Education.

ROSS, L. and L. J. CRONBACH [eds.] (1976) "Evaluating the Handbook of Evaluation Research," pp. 195-218 in G. V. Glass (ed.) Evaluation Studies Review Annual, Volume 1. Beverly Hills: Sage Publications.

SCRIVEN, M. (1967) "The methodology of evaluation," pp. 39-83 in R. E. Stake (ed.) Perspectives of Curriculum Evaluation. AERA Monograph Series on Curriculum Evaluation, No. 1. Chicago: Rand McNally.

SJOBERG, G. (1975) "Politics, ethics and evaluation research," pp. 29-54 in M. Guttentag and E. L. Struening (eds.) Handbook of Evaluation Research, Volume 2. Beverly Hills: Sage Publications.

SMITH, L. M. (in press) "An evolving logic of participant observation, educational ethnography and other case studies," in L. Shulman (ed.) Review of Research in Education, Volume 6. Chicago: Peacock.

STAKE, R. (1978) "The case study method in social inquiry." Educational Researcher (February).

STOUT, R. (1978) "Education and the quest for control of public programs." PASITAM Newsletter (Indiana University, Bloomington) 18 (Summer).

Thomas J. Kiresuk
and
Sander H. Lund
Program Evaluation
Resource Center

3

PROGRAM EVALUATION AND
UTILIZATION ANALYSIS

INTRODUCTION

The purpose of this chapter is to help clarify the conceptual and operational links among the fields of knowledge transfer, planned change and evaluative research, showing how the three interact to form central elements in the larger enterprise of knowledge utilization. Particular emphasis will be accorded to the role of evaluation in knowledge utilization, and specific suggestions will be made as to how knowledge utilization concepts can be brought into routine and active inclusion in evaluation activities.

THE BACKGROUND OF KNOWLEDGE UTILIZATION

Knowledge utilization, the study and practice of facilitating development, dissemination and use of information, finds its origins in the widely recognized difficulty of putting valid scientific knowledge to constructive social use. The Battelle Columbus Laboratories (National Science Foundation, 1973), for example, have determined that the average time lag between discovery and systematic use of ten major technical inventions was nearly twenty years. In education, Miles (1965) has estimated that the average latency between conception and adoption of new ideas is thirty years. Since, as Glaser and Marks (1966) observe, "It is destructive and wasteful that people should be frustrated and often defeated by difficulties for which someone else has already found a remedy," it is no surprise that scientists and practitioners alike are seeking means to bridge the gap between what one writer (Joly, 1967) has called "the two solitudes of research and practice."

Because of their central relevance to almost all areas of applied science, knowledge utilization concepts have been investigated in many fields of inquiry: anthropology (Barnett, 1953), sociology (Hage and Aiken, 1970), agriculture (Fliegel and Kivlin, 1966), medicine (Coleman, Katz, and Menzel, 1966), public health (Mytinger, 1968), business administration (Becker and Whisler, 1967), communications (Katz, Levin, and Hamilton, 1963), political science (Mohr, 1969), and economics (Mansfield, 1963). In recent years, the volume, quality, and diversity of this study have led to attempts to integrate knowledge utilization ideas and findings into a manageable set of concepts and/or action principles. The literature distillations of Rogers (1962), Rogers and Shoemaker (1971), Rothman (1974), and the Human Interaction Research Institute (1976) have been enormously important in defining the parameters and explicating the central concepts of knowledge utilization.

EVALUATION AS A KNOWLEDGE UTILIZATION CONCEPT

The maturation of knowledge utilization and the integration of ideas from diverse fields of inquiry have led to growing recognition of the importance of evaluation research as a means to develop, assess, and promote new ideas. The pioneering effort in this regard has been that of Howard Davis, Chief of the Mental Health Services Development Branch of the National Institute of Mental Health. For more than two decades, Davis has pointed to the minimal impact of evaluation findings on clinical, program, and policy decision-making, and has argued that the program evaluator occupies a unique position to serve as a "change agent" in the stimulation and facilitation of constructive innovation. As the evaluation field has evolved, concern over nonutilization of evaluation results has prompted a growing number of others to join with Davis. Michael Patton, for example, has recently published a book entitled *Utilization—Focused Evaluation,* which presents specific techniques to maximize the impact of evaluation, and *Evaluation* magazine has changed its title to *Evaluation and Change,* demonstrating its editorial recognition of the fundamental link between these two concepts. Weiss (1972), Glaser (1973), Caplan (1975), Knorr (1977), Rich (1977), Larsen (1978a), and a host of others are making exciting contributions toward reducing the barriers between the production and use of knowledge.

Kiresuk, Davis, and Lund (in press) argue that the defining ingredients in knowledge utilization are "knowledge transfer" (communicating new ideas from developers to users), "planned change" (facilitating the adoption of new ideas), and "evaluation research." In this context evaluation has two roles, serving both as the means to create knowledge and as the means to assess the effectiveness of its use. Thus, although the blending of evaluation and knowledge utilization may seem problematic at first, it seems clear that they have many attributes in common. Further evidence of this is indicated by the routine, though sometimes implicit, inclusion of evaluation concepts in most knowledge utilization models.

Evaluation in the Research and Development Process

Six general conceptual models exist relevant to the knowledge utilization process (Human Interaction Research Institute, 1976). In each of these some form of evaluation plays a prominent part.

Research, development, and diffusion model. According to the research development and diffusion model (Havelock, 1969), knowledge utilization is conceptualized as a rational and orderly sequence of three stages: (1) determination of a research need, (2) development of a solution to the need, and (3) dissemination of the solution to a passively receptive audience. Acceptance of the knowledge is assured by correct timing and appropriate packaging. The role of evaluation in this process is to assure the quality and acceptability of the innovation, and to guide the diffusion process.

Social interaction model. In this model (Havelock, 1969), an appropriate base of knowledge is assumed, and emphasis is placed on stimulating the receptiveness of potential audiences. This is accomplished by implementing appropriate "influencing strategies" at each stage of the R & D process, rather than waiting until the research is complete. Here the evaluation takes the form of consumer testing of an innovation prior to adoption.

Problem-solving model. The emphasis in this model (Havelock, 1969) is on the psychological workings of potential adopters. Based on the assumption that self-initiated change has the firmest motivation, the problem solving model specifies use of a change agent who uses nondirective techniques to facilitate potential adopters use of their own decision-making resources. The examination of various possible solutions would involve the use of evaluation findings, and would be a form of evaluation itself.

Planned change model. Elaborating on the problem solving model, the planned changed model (Sashkin, Morris, and Horst, 1973) emphasizes the need for cooperation between change agent and client in the development and implementation of new ideas. In this view, information is regarded as useful only if it leads to positive action, and the client involved in evaluating the need for the change and in evaluating the change itself.

Action research model. Lewin's action research model, as explicated by Sashkin, Morris, and Horst (1973), follows the same dynamic as the planned change model, but places stronger emphasis on the institutionalization of research and development technology in particular organizations. Action research is seen as an on-going function intended to identify and address important organizational problems and the basic assumption is that research and development is a continuous cycle of inquiry, innovation, evaluation, and further inquiry.

Decision Determinants Analysis

The point of this review of established R & D models has been to emphasize that even if it is not labeled as such, evaluation has always played a central role in knowledge utilization activities. Recognition of this fact is spreading, and evaluation methods are becoming a formal component of systematic strategies to facilitate organizational innovation. One such strategy is Decision Determinants Analysis (DDA), a consultation strategy developed to rationalize the organizational change process without excluding nonrational concerns (Davis and Salasin, 1975). As can be seen in Figure 1, DDA has an explicit evaluation orientation: needs are identified, goals are formulated to meet the needs, action steps are developed to attain the goals, goal attainment is used to evaluate the action steps, and evaluation feedback is used as corrective feedback. In DDA, evaluation assessment takes two forms: before the change the A VICTORY model (Davis, 1973) is used to assess readiness for innovation; and after the change, Goal Attainment Scaling (Kiresuk and Sherman, 1968) is used to determine success.

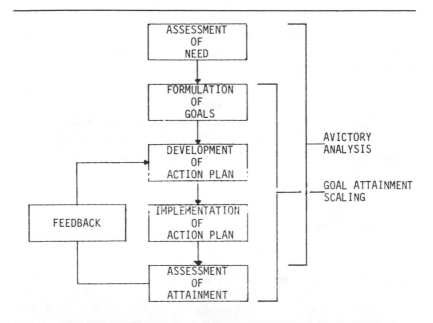

Figure 1: Process and Elements in the Decision Determinants Analysis (DDA) Planned Change Consultation Model

KNOWLEDGE UTILIZATION AS AN
EVALUATION CONCEPT

If evaluation is a common concept in knowledge utilization, what about the converse: to what extent can knowledge utilization concepts be found in the evaluation literature? Only a slight substitution of concepts is required in many cases.

Resistance to Evaluation

Probably the most common and familiar experience among evaluators is the opposition they encounter in implementing their methods. All too often methodologically sound research methods, measurement devices and information systems are rejected or improperly implemented owing to seemingly irrational resistance. It is instructive and perhaps comforting to recognize that knowledge utilization has long been concerned with this topic. For example, intense scrutiny has been leveled at the time lag between conception and adoption of innovations, and mechanisms are being developed to facilitate the effective transfer of knowledge from developers to users (Havelock, 1968; Rothman, 1974). Attention has also been accorded to resistance at the programmatic and individual level, and many techniques to dispel or at least mitigate unnecessary opposition to change are being developed and tested (Lewis, 1962; Lippitt and Fox, 1967; Hoveland, Janis, and Kelley, 1953). Those who wish distinguished company in the battle against resistance to wholesome ideas need only recall the struggles of Semmelweis (Thompson, 1954) in convincing physicians to wash their hands prior to surgery and to have the sheets changed in maternity wards. Researchers and evaluators in all spheres soon recognize that no matter how technically compelling the evidence, change is rarely stimulated by information alone.

The Durability of Evaluation

Means to assure the durability of evaluation methods have been discussed by many writers. Glaser and Backer (1977) suggest that one means to reduce resistance to an evaluation method is to "re-invent" it in each new setting; to make appropriate alterations in the basic design so that it fits comfortably with the setting's unique needs and constraints. This tends not only to enhance its compatibility with a new mileau, but can catalyze commitment by building pride and encouraging a sense of ownership.

"Re-invention" is not universally regarded as a positive process. Calsyn, Tornatzky, and Dittmar (1977) content that under the guise of tailoring an idea to suit a new setting its technical quality may be seriously impaired. Recommending that the integration of an innovation be safeguarded by making implementation the responsibility of an outside technical expert, these authors are forthright in their recommendations: "the change agent has an obligation to protest vigorously any modifications in the innovation that would compromise its effectiveness."

A third position in the re-invention debate is presented by Larsen and Agarwala-Rogers (1977). Pointing out that uncritical acceptance of an innovation assures transfer of negative as well as positive features, Larsen and Agarwala-Rogers recommend that an "innovation be introduced as a general concept and include recommendations to facilitate appropriate re-invention in a local setting so as to help fit local conditions and make the innovation more acceptable to users."

The importance of evaluation as a means to organizational change should not prevent recognition that it is also a form of organizational change. The same knowledge transfer and planned change techniques that can be used to enhance the utilization of evaluation results can also serve to facilitate installation of evaluation. As the controversy surrounding the concept of re-invention demonstrates, implementation of evaluation is a form of planned change that is often the inescapable responsibility of evaluation experts. Success in this requires them to act as change agents whether they recognize this role or not.

Utilization of Results

The current search for means to enhance the impact of evaluation on clinical, program and policy decision-making provides other examples of the importance of knowledge utilization concepts to successful evaluation. Consideration of the questions "how does one make evaluation relevant?" and "how does one promote the utilization of evaluation results?" takes evaluators out of a narrowly defined technical role and requires them to attend to a full range of knowledge transfer and planned change issues. An evaluator must be able to identify the real audience of an evaluation, segment the audience into its major components, and tailor the evaluation to meet the information needs of each (Zaltman and Duncan, 1977). Evaluators must be able to conduct a systematic prior assessment of the program to be evaluated, and develop and evaluation design appropriate to local conditions. Evaluators must be able to anticipate sources of resistance and move to disarm them (Rogers and Shoemaker, 1971). In determining the success of an evaluation effort, design and measurement issues are often trivial in comparison with developing means for the smooth implementation of the design and effective dissemination of results.

Formative Evaluation

"Formative evaluation," (Scriven, 1972) is another evaluation concept with direct relevance to knowledge utilization. In Scriven's view, formative evaluation is a form of assessment intended to provide corrective feedback for the improvement of established programs, and is distinguished from "summative evaluation," whose purpose is to determine if a new and untried program is worth continuing. Although both processes are aimed at production of knowledge for decision-making, formative evaluation is especially germane to this discussion because its focus on the use of feedback as a basis for organizational change helps to explicate the nature of evaluation as a knowledge transfer process. Like the research and development processes described previously, formative evaluation must be undertaken consonant with knowledge utilization principles and techniques: the inquiry must be initiated with target questions in mind, the results must be transferred to decision-makers in a way that facilitates action; the utilization of results typically requires planned change activities.

"Reforms as Experiments"

Although the rephrasing of individual evaluation concepts and activities into knowledge utilization parlance could proceed at length, such a process could never match the elegance and incisiveness already demonstrated by Donald T. Campbell (1972) in his seminal essay "Reforms as Experiments." Emphasizing the interdependence of evaluation research and social change, Campbell's discussion centers on means to use social reforms as policy experiments, but is also a systematic analysis of the ways in which valid knowledge can be used as a basis for needed innovation. The entire work represents an effort to adapt the traditional methods of scientific inquiry to the social and political realities of applied research and evaluation settings, with Campbell (acting as a good change agent) helping to adapt social research methodology so that it is acceptable to practitioners and consumers. Certainly Campbell's sensitivity to the thoughts and feelings of "trapped administrators" and his awareness of the vicissitudes of public life indicate a recognition of the need to accommodate contextual factors in the conduct of social inquiry. This recognition parallels the basic intent of the problem solving, planned change, and action research models described previously.

KNOWLEDGE UTILIZATION PRINCIPLES FOR EVALUATION RESEARCH

Even if elements of knowledge utilization can be found in the enterprise of evaluation research, what practical and tangible benefit can there be to the evaluator in calling attention to this commonality? The second portion of this chapter is devoted to illustrating the practical relevance of knowledge utilization principles to the basic program evaluation process.

Assessment of Readiness for Evaluation

It is accepted practice in most approaches to program evaluation to conduct a prior analysis of the organization to determine its actual nature and intent. Joseph Wholey (1977), for example, recommends an "evaluability assessment" to determine the extent to which a viable program with answerable questions actually exists. In "Goal Free Evaluation" (Scriven, 1974) the purpose of this assessment is to ferret out the real, rather than the putative, purposes of the organization. In "Utilization-Focused Evaluation" (Patton, 1978) the function is to determine the information needs of specific decision-makers. Often involving client surveys, staff and leadership interviews, and examination of records, the intent of such analyses is specification of criteria by which organizational success will be determined. Incorporation of knowledge utilization principles into this process would involve two additional procedures: (1) an analysis of the readiness of the organization to accept the changes which may be suggested by the evaluation.

THE A VICTORY MEASURE OF ORGANIZATIONAL
READINESS FOR EVALUATION

Many theories, models and typologies are available for organizatinal analyses of readiness for change. Four of these are presented in Figure 2: Glaser's CORRECT acronym (1973); Havelock and Lingwood's (1973) HELP-SCORE acronym; Zaltman, Duncan, and Holbek's list of innovation attributes (1973); and Davis's A VICTORY formulation. As can be seen, there is a high level of comparability in these models, and seemingly any of them would provide an excellent base for the construction of a "readiness for evaluation" measure.

The Program Evaluation Resource Center in Minneapolis, Minnesota, is currently developing a measure of organizational readiness for program evaluation. Because of our prior experience with the A VICTORY model, it has been selected as the

"AVICTORY" (H. Davis)	"CORRECT" (E. Glaser)	"Innovation Attributes" (Zaltman, et al.)	"HELP-SCORE" (Havelock and Lingwood)
Ability to carry out the change	Capability & Resources	Financial & Social Costs	Structuring Capacity
Values or self-expectancy	Compatability	Compatability Publicness vs. Privateness Impact on Interpersonal relations	Homophily Empathy
Idea or information about the innovation.	Credibility Ease in understanding & installation Observability Triability Divisibility Reversibility	Communicability Divisibility Reversibility Complexity Modifiability Scientific Status Point of Origin Terminability	Openness
Circumstances which prevail at the time.	Openness to challenge Climate of trust Structural reorganization.		Proximity
Timing or readiness to consider the idea.	Sensitivity to context factors Early involvement of users. Suitable timing		Linking Synergy
Obligation or felt need to change	Relevance Widespread felt need for change. Shared interest in problem solving	Degree of commitment	Energy
Resistance or inhibiting factors	Skill in working through resistances	Risks or uncertainty Number of gatekeepers or approval channels	
Yield, or perceived payoff	Relative advantage Incentive system	Efficiency of innovation Relative advantage Gateway of other innovations	Reward

Figure 2: Factors Influencing the Implementation of an Innovation by an Organization: Four Formulations (adopted from HIRI, 1976)

framework for this effort. A VICTORY has a plausible rationale, seems to encompass all of the salient characteristics in the existing literature, and is relatively easy to convert into empirical indicators. The eight factors in the A VICTORY acronym are:

Ability: Availability or accessibility of the material, personnel or financial resources necessary for change.

Values: The congeniality to innovation of the organizations' prevailing norms and philosophy.

Information: Quality and credibility of the innovation and availability of information sufficient to implement it.

Circumstances: Stable environmental and organizational attributes influencing change.

Timing: Dynamic environmental and organizational factors influencing change.

Obligation: Degree of pressure, or "felt need," to implement the innovation.

Resistance: Degree of opposition to the change; existence and strength of inhibitors.

Yield: The probable outcome of the innovation; the intended and unintended benefits and losses.

The questionnaire consists of 85 opinion statements, which are rated by a respondent in accordance with a four point scale of agreement or disagreement. Results are reported in the form of scores on each of 14 A VICTORY scales and subscales (Figure 3). Such scores are interpreted according to the range of scores possible on that scale. According to Mayer (1975), who was responsible for development of the scoring procedures, "this form of testing (called 'domain referenced' as opposed to the more traditional 'norm referenced') yields scores that . . . are more interpretable; one can make judgments about an organization's readiness without having to know how other organizations typically score." Scoring and interpretation of the instrument is automated: the range of each scale is divided into equal quarters and predetermined interpretations are printed out according to the quarter occupied by the subject organization. At the present time, the A VICTORY instrument is completed by several members of a subject organization, and it is asked that respondents represent a "good mix" of job titles and responsibilities.

Using this measure one can perform an analysis of the host organization regarding its receptivity to the proposed evaluation method. Early applications of the measure, done during its development phase, suggest the type of analysis of which it may be capable. Remembering that the measure is in revision, and has

ABILITY

    Category 1:   Willingness and ability to commit resources to program evalutation.

    Category 2:   Present availability and skill level of manpower to plan and implement program evaluation. Knowlege level regarding program evaluation of those concerned.

VALUES

    Category 3:   Attitudes and beliefs of those involved toward accepting program evaluation.

    Category 4:   Organization's history of change and history of support for change.

    Category 5:   Characteristics of staff or administrators thought to bear on acceptance of program evaluation (other than skill level).

    Category 6:   Work relations; supervisory relations; interpersonal relations.

    Category 7:   Employment or personnel policies of the organization (i.e., of the employer).

INFORMATION

    Category 8:   Availability of information bearing on program's present functioning. Availability and use of procedures and channels for recording and communicating program information.

CIRCUMSTANCES

    Category 9:   Aspects of the program relating to procedures, job duties, job requirements, and job expectations.

    Category 10:   Quality of relationships between the program and those it serves and works with.

TIMING

    Category 11:   Timing of the program evaluation to coincide or coordinate with other program or organizational activities.

Figure 3: AVICTORY Dimensions for Organizational Assessment of Readiness to Implement Program Evaluation

OBLIGATION

    Category 12: Felt need to 'do something,' to take action.
                    Pressure to evaluate. Awareness of present
                    health of the organization.

RESISTANCE

    Category 13: Expected or feared negative consequences of
                    program evaluation. Frontstage or backstage
                    fears of loss resulting from adoption of
                    program evaluation.

YIELD

    Category 14: Expected or hoped for positive consequences of
                    program evaluation. Payoff or rewards thought
                    to result from program evaluation.

Figure 3 (Continued)

been the subject of only research reports (Studer, 1978; Gianetti, Johnson, and Williams, 1978); the results are at least provocative. The data below are from an A VICTORY analysis done regarding the implementation of Goal Attainment Scaling in a Canadian psychiatric penitentiary (Kiresuk and Lund, in press.)

A CASE STUDY

Figure 4, the results of an overall A VICTORY analysis of the organization prior to implementation of Goal Attainment Scaling, suggest that in this setting GAS was compatible with prevailing values, but might be resisted because of the way change had been attempted in the past and because of current employment conditions. Notice that any inclination on the part of the evaluator to argue on behalf of GAS, or to tinker with its characteristics in order to make it more palatable, would totally miss this point of opposition.

Subdividing by staff discipline provided profiles suggesting different patterns of resistance (Figure 5). Psychologists and psychiatrists were generally in favor of Goal Attainment Scaling, but were not willing to invest time in its implementation. Social workers, on the other hand, manifested a very high compatibility of values with the innovation, but also felt a very low pressure to

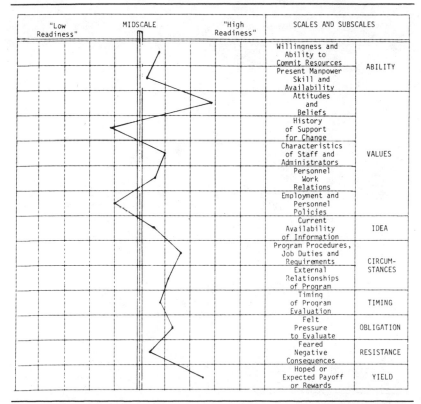

"Low Readiness"	MIDSCALE	"High Readiness"	SCALES AND SUBSCALES	
			Willingness and Ability to Commit Resources	ABILITY
			Present Manpower Skill and Availability	
			Attitudes and Beliefs	
			History of Support for Change	
			Characteristics of Staff and Administrators	VALUES
			Personnel Work Relations	
			Employment and Personnel Policies	
			Current Availability of Information	IDEA
			Program Procedures, Job Duties and Requirements	CIRCUM-STANCES
			External Relationships of Program	
			Timing of Program Evaluation	TIMING
			Felt Pressure to Evaluate	OBLIGATION
			Feared Negative Consequences	RESISTANCE
			Hoped or Expected Payoff or Rewards	YIELD

Figure 4: AVICTORY Profile Results for Staff of Canadian Psychiatric Prison (N=45)

evaluate. Obviously a special strategy would be required to influence the adoptive readiness of the social work department. While they express many opinions in common with the total program, their lack of a sense of obligation to participate would seem to require special sensitization to the need for a program evaluation system.

On the level of individual staff, Figure 6 is the profile of a person with a positive orientation to the implementation of Goal Attainment Scaling. Such a person might serve as an "internal champion" of the innovation, facilitating its adoption and providing a natural rallying point for those who favor the idea. Figure 7 is the profile of a person with a negative orientation

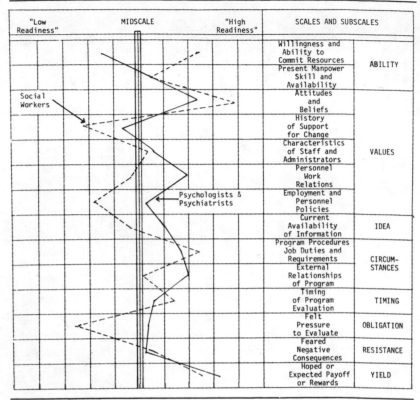

"Low Readiness"	MIDSCALE	"High Readiness"	SCALES AND SUBSCALES	
			Willingness and Ability to Commit Resources	ABILITY
			Present Manpower Skill and Availability	
Social Workers			Attitudes and Beliefs	VALUES
			History of Support for Change	
			Characteristics of Staff and Administrators	
			Personnel Work Relations	
	Psychologists & Psychiatrists		Employment and Personnel Policies	
			Current Availability of Information	IDEA
			Program Procedures Job Duties and Requirements	CIRCUM- STANCES
			External Relationships of Program	
			Timing of Program Evaluation	TIMING
			Felt Pressure to Evaluate	OBLIGATION
			Feared Negative Consequences	RESISTANCE
			Hoped or Expected Payoff or Rewards	YIELD

Figure 5: AVICTORY Profile Results for Two Disciplines of a Canadian Psychiatric Prison

toward Goal Attainment Scaling. The profile has so many low points, some special to this staff person and some consonant with the opinions of the total program, that a host of techniques would be necessary in order to bring about change. At the most extreme level, such persons might be worked around, or left until last in the change process. The contrast between the two staff members is interesting. Both have favorable attitudes and beliefs, but one feels coercion to implement an unwanted change, while the other wants to implement a change for which there is no perceived pressure. No wonder that simple exhortation and education are so marginally effective in facilitating innovation.

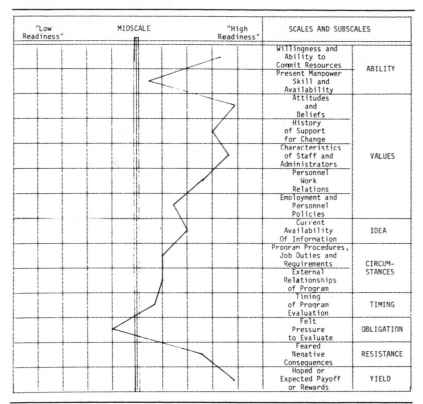

"Low Readiness"					MIDSCALE					"High Readiness"		SCALES AND SUBSCALES	
												Willingness and Ability to Commit Resources	ABILITY
												Present Manpower Skill and Availability	
												Attitudes and Beliefs	VALUES
												History of Support for Change	
												Characteristics of Staff and Administrators	
												Personnel Work Relations	
												Employment and Personnel Policies	
												Current Availability Of Information	IDEA
												Program Procedures, Job Duties and Requirements	CIRCUM-STANCES
												External Relationships of Program	
												Timing of Program Evaluation	TIMING
												Felt Pressure to Evaluate	OBLIGATION
												Feared Negative Consequences	RESISTANCE
												Hoped or Expected Payoff or Rewards	YIELD

Figure 6: AVICTORY Profile Results for "Internal Champion" of Change in a Canadian Psychiatric Prison

Although the early applications of the A VICTORY measure have provided interesting descriptive information, caution should be exercised in its general use, particularly as regards individual staff interpretations. The initial version has only been administered to a few hundred self-selected organizations, and the test has a long way to go to meet accepted psychometric standards. However, revisions are being made, norms are being developed, and various measures of validity and reliability are being taken. In addition, the model is being elaborated by other investigators using different models (Larsen, 1978b; Strommen, 1978; Glaser, 1973; Salasin and Davis, 1977), and work is also proceeding on other planned change models (Havelock and

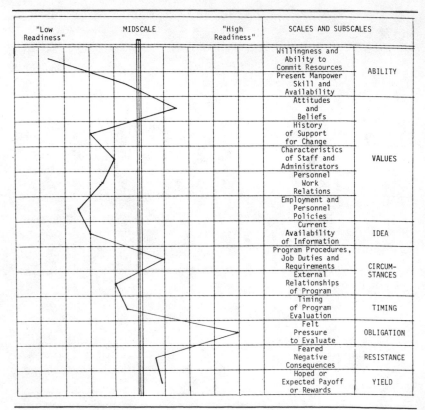

"Low Readiness"	MIDSCALE	"High Readiness"	SCALES AND SUBSCALES	
			Willingness and Ability to Commit Resources	ABILITY
			Present Manpower Skill and Availability	
			Attitudes and Beliefs	VALUES
			History of Support for Change	
			Characteristics of Staff and Administrators	
			Personnel Work Relations	
			Employment and Personnel Policies	
			Current Availability of Information	IDEA
			Program Procedures, Job Duties and Requirements	CIRCUM-STANCES
			External Relationships of Program	
			Timing of Program Evaluation	TIMING
			Felt Pressure to Evaluate	OBLIGATION
			Feared Negative Consequences	RESISTANCE
			Hoped or Expected Payoff or Rewards	YIELD

Figure 7: A VICTORY Profile of Individual "High Resister" of Change in a Canadian Psychiatric Prison

Lingwood, 1973). At the very least the findings educed thus far illustrate the kinds of concepts that could be brought forth in both the descriptive and prescriptive stages of planned organizational change.

FUTURE DIRECTIONS

Assuming that the questionnaire does prove to be an acceptable measure of organizational readiness for program evaluation, what are the directions for future development? One strategy might be to develop a companion measure to assess the "acceptability" of specific innovations. Glaser's CORRECT acronym would be an excellent starting point for this project. Another strategy would be to construct a measure of the appropriateness of particular implementation strategies, perhaps using the planned change schema promulgated by Chin and Benne (1969). Taken as a package, such a battery of measures would permit development of change strategies tailored not only to the organization undergoing change, but to the innovation itself, and to the proposed implementation strategy.

Implementation Strategies

At this time there is only a little in the planned change literature that is of practical benefit to those implementing evaluation. Fairweather, Sanders, and Tornatzky (1974) recommend "active" intervention styles (i.e., pressure from outside agent combined with support from a corps of internal change advocates), while Bonoma (1977) argues that the implementation strategy should be determined by the balance of power between those who support and oppose evaluation in an organization. In a recent article describing the implementation of Goal Attainment Scaling in a Canadian penitentiary (Kiresuk and Lund, in press), Howard Davis has provided a list of implementation suggestions based on an A VICTORY analysis of the host organization (Figure 8). Overall, there is much accumulated wisdom and a wealth of helpful suggestions in the literature, and many skilled consultants are available, but the stage of inquiry is very early, perhaps corresponding to the early stages of the psychotherapy movement.

Zaltman and Duncan (1977) have described and listed an array of methods and techniques for facilitating planned change, but the systematic research necessary to validate these ideas has not been done. The research process would parallel that of psychotherapy: the treatment itself must be defined so it can be replicated; the innovation (desired outcome) has to be specified; the characteristics of the setting must be controlled; consultant characteristics must be studied.

Eventually it should be possible to match diagnoses and treatment for specific organizational problems, determining which treatment is necessary for which problem, with what expected

1. Work with the source of greatest resistance first; talk it over, allowing for ventilation and clarification. Resistance at this point can be reduced by allowing technical modifications in the innovation.

2. Identify internal zealots who can assist in carrying through the innovation. Capitalize on potential champions of change: these will be younger or older than average, intelligent, not members of the organizational elite, and somewhat socially isolated.

3. Try the innovation on a trial basis in a unit where it seems most likely to succeed. Reward success conspicuously.

4. Use peer pressure and reinforcement to support change: get internal opinion leaders to accept the innovation.

5. "Re-invention," changing the innovation so that it seems to be invented at the target program, is often a useful strategy to bring about organizational change.

6. Look at the whole program. Put effort and resources where change is most likely. Leave laggard units until last.

7. Examine motivation for change. Some individuals and program elements are preconditioned for innovation. Exploit this.

8. If change is unlikely to be successful, don't attempt it. It is better not to try, than to try and fail. Failure can reinforce resistance to change, and make subsequent attempts even more difficult.

9. If GAS is being used to evaluate and monitor the innovation effort, exploit its potential for rewards: attainment of "Better Than Expected" or "Best Anticipated" outcomes should be reinforced lavishly.

10. If there is low perception of need for the innovation, conduct targeted interviews to determine why.

11. Be judicious in using participative decision-making. Staff involvement can often reduce resistance, but in authoritarian organizations can be interperted as indecision. Sometimes it is better to just push on through.

12. Segmentalize the groups involved in the innovation, identifying and addressing the unique needs of each segment.

Figure 8: General Principles for Implementing Program Evaluation

outcome and at what cost. For the present however, in the absence of a firm research base, it is comforting that most of the concepts involved are straightforward, face validity is easily achieved, consumer satisfaction is usually high, and the "treatments" are often self-evident. For instance, if certain components of an organization lack information on evaluation, it would simply be supplied to them. As this shows, a major accomplishment in the current literature has been the sectioning of previously amorphous obstacles to planned change into discrete and manageable components.

Until this point in the discussion it has been implicitly assumed that adoption of new ideas requires modifications in individuals and organizations accomplished through planned change "treatments." It is equally possible, however, that the innovation itself might require alteration. The interpretation of an "organizational readiness for evaluation" profile might be different for evaluation methods with differing characteristics. It is probable, for instance, that organizations already using Management by Objectives would be largely receptive to goal-oriented evaluation systems, while organizations with established standardized assessment systems might find goal setting unnatural or inappropriate. Altering the evaluation system to improve its compatibility with organizational characteristics might lead to a quicker and more enduring adoption.

Concern regarding spontaneous modifications in an evaluation system is a related issue. A frequent implementation strategy is to regard a proposed evaluation system as sacrosanct, reacting to all deviations as though they are error variance intruding on an optimal solution. Research in this area, however, has suggested that such modifications are almost inevitable (Larsen and Agarwala-Rogers, 1977), a reality that is often unrecognized if the investigator insists that the initial system be implemented completely intact. Apparent resistance may mean that a proposed change is not workable (Spicer, 1952) or that it has effects that were not anticipated (Miles, 1965). Instead of dogmatically attempting to stamp out all deviation, the evaluator should respond flexibly to such impulses, using them as means to blend the needs of the design with the needs of the host organization. Close attention to the sources and nature of desire for modifications in an evaluation can provide invaluable information for improving the basic conception and tailoring it to fit comfortably in a given setting.

Longitudinal Assessment of Change

The analyses described thus far are simple cross-sectional studies involving diagnosis of the organization and development of an appropriate implementation plan. The image of planned change presented by such analyses is static, like a photograph, and is unlike the flowing interaction of events which occurs in the real world. As Zaltman, Duncan, and Holbek (1973) argue, innovation is a dynamic process, not an isolated event, taking different forms at different times and requiring different interventions at each stage of the adoptive process. While individual cross-sectional analyses are revealing, full understanding of planned change will require longitudinal designs. A hypothetical example of such a design is presented in Figure 9. Note that the A VICTORY factors ebb and flow as time passes, each having its own periodicity. Across the top of the diagram are the major concurrent events that are believed to influence the function curves of the A VICTORY dimensions. "Implementation of MBO," for example, enhances Values and reduces Resistance, while "Reception of Grant" simultaneously elevates Ability and Obligation. Below the graph is the adoption curve of the innovation, showing the degree to which compliance with the new practice varies over time. Notice that success in institutionalizing the innovation begins to decay after the first burst of success, indicating the need for periodic booster applications of support.

Measurement of Knowledge Utilization

What are the design and measurement implications of knowledge utilization analysis? The beginning point would be determining the probable reception of a new idea through parallel assessments of (1) organizational readiness to change, (2) com-

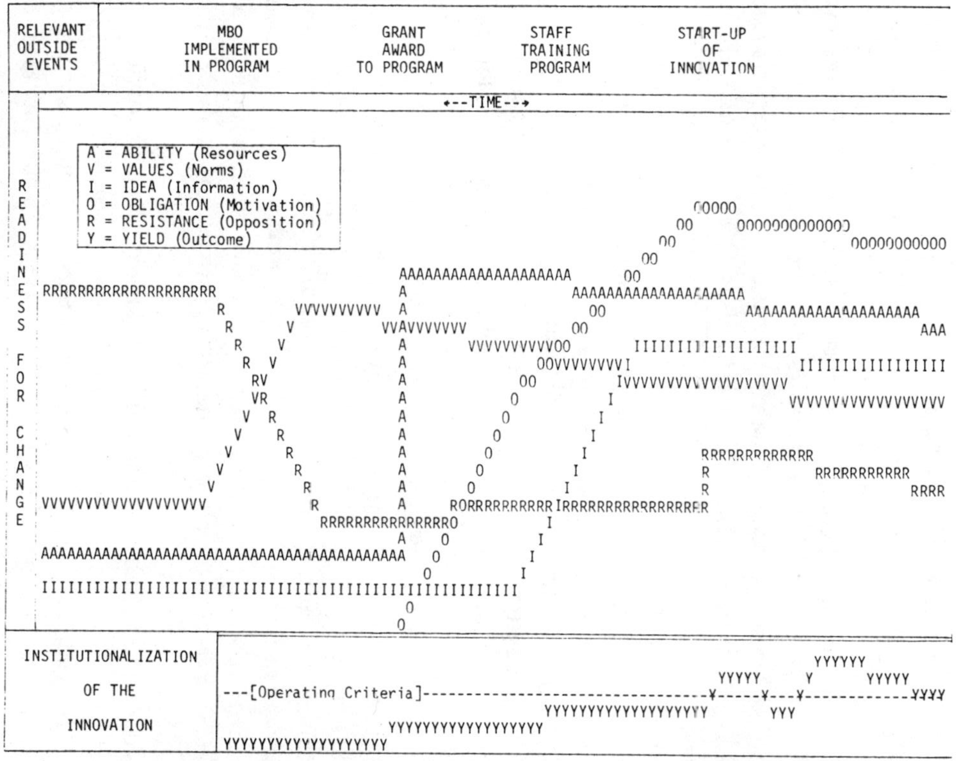

Figure 9: Hypothetical Example of Variation in AVICTORY Factors During the Implementation of Evaluation

patibility of the idea to the host organization, and (3) appropriateness of the selected knowledge transfer and planned change strategies. Such analyses could be carried out at the policy level, the program level or the level of individual human beings.

Coordinated change analyses, for example, could be conducted as part of the implementation of Quality Assurance technology in the national system of community mental health centers. The first step would be to ascertain the readiness of the system when the concept was first proposed. This would involve A VICTORY surveys to determine how organizations and professional groups perceive Quality Assurance, and could also involve use of the CORRECT or HELP-SCORE formulations to determine the "transferability" of the fundamental Quality Assurance model.

Knowing the results of these assessments, specific knowledge transfer and planned change strategies could be targeted to each discipline and to typical organizational profile types. Quality Assurance information could then be disseminated in forms specially formulated for individual professional disciplines. Organizational and governmental policies could be altered to provide special rewards for those involved in the Quality Assurance process. Ability to comply with Quality Assurance requirements could be assured through grants or cost sharing agreements. Resistances in the form of apprehension at trying something new could be mitigated through training programs. An attempt could be made to match Quality Assurance models with certain CORRECT characteristics to organizations with certain A VICTORY profiles.

Although the above scenario is only illustrative, it provides an outline of how a readiness analysis could proceed in a complex and dynamic system. A VICTORY concepts could be used both to organize a historical review and to assess the current status of an innovation. In the absence of adequate quantification, the concepts would serve as a conceptual guide for review of topics that have a self-evident quality in decision-making.

An additional variable that influences the success of efforts at planned change is the energy and skill invested in the implementation strategy. Just as a treatment implemented halfheartedly will not have the same effect as a treatment implemented enthusiastically, a treatment implemented in strict compliance with a planned change strategy will not have the same effect as one implementated in a lackadaisical manner (Rossi, Freeman, and Wright, 1979). Perhaps the studies of the relative effectiveness of educational, mental health, and other treatments could benefit from similar analyses. This would involve determining the readiness of service providers to give a treatment, as well as the readiness of clients to comply with it.

Patient Compliance with Treatment

At the client level, knowledge utilization analysis takes the form of finding means to facilitate patient compliance with treatment recommendations. This would involve finding means to assure that necessary information is effectively exchanged between clinician and client, and the obstacles to patient compliance are remedied. Susan Schultz, of the Program Evaluation Resource Center, is currently developing an A VICTORY measure of client readiness to accept medical treatment. A sample profile from this measure is provided in Figure 10. An intriguing possibility with such analyses is to try to link compliance measures with measures of treatment effectiveness. If successful this would lead to matching of treatment and subject in order to maximize outcomes.

Research Quality Assurance

Another application of knowledge utilization analysis would be a quality assurance mechanism for the research process. Monitoring the nature of the treatments actually provided, making certain randomization is being carried out and assuring that the research protocol is being followed are central tasks in dealing with threats to internal and external validity. One means to facilitate this would be an analysis to determine the readiness

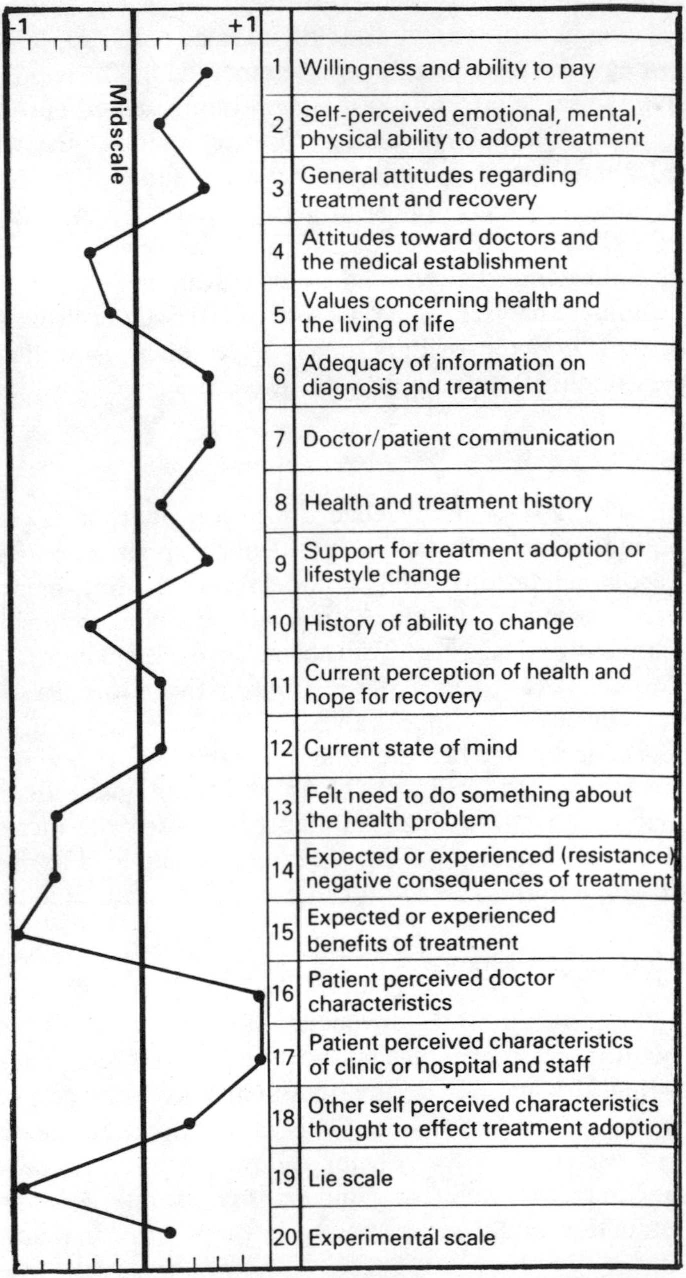

Figure 10: Sample Patient Readiness Profile

of therapists to administer the treatment being studied. It might also be possible to study the readiness of therapists and other staff to comply with experimental conditions. The erosion of results due to "human factors" that occurs in all applied research could be remedied through knowledge utilization analysis rather than being accepted as an unavoidable research error.

FUTURE DIRECTIONS

To be sure this has only been a conceptual overview and much work remains to bring these ideas to full fruition, but the essentials are clear. Future development of the knowledge utilization field would involve at least the following tasks: (1) development of systematic theories of knowledge utilization, (2) construction of measures of organizational readiness to change, (3) construction of measures of the "transferability" of particular innovations, (4) specification of strategies to determine the degree of institutionalization of an innovation, (5) development of research designs to investigate the planned change process, and (6) development of change interventions and testing them.

In addition, of course, the overall knowledge utilization process itself must be evaluated. Designs have been developed in both administrative and clinical settings to test the impact of presence or absence of A VICTORY analyses in the hands of administrators or therapists. The analyses themselves are thus treated as forms of intervention and compared with other forms of intervention. It is expected that there may be a treatment facilitation effect contributing to clinical and administrative outcomes.

This outline of the essentials of knowledge utilization analysis is in varying stages of implementation. Progress to date suggests that the methods are feasible, well received, and have general applicability. While our interest in the area was prompted by our concern about improving the outcome of human service treatments to individual recipients, the concepts have found ready application to larger organizational units and appear promising for large-scale adoption.

The effort to incorporate planned change technology within evaluative research proceeds with full awareness of the unease it may arouse in the evaluation community. Robert Stake has argued forcefully that there is nothing inherent in the role of evaluator which permits or legitimates assumption of responsibility for advocation of change. Noting threats to the validity of evaluation designs, Selma Mushkin (1973) has expressed concern that the technical quality of evaluation information is often insufficient for programmatic and policy decision-making. In a recent survey the readers of *Evaluation and Change* magazine have expressed doubts that evaluators have skills and knowledge sufficient to act as change agents.

Although these and related concerns must be addressed before change advocacy can be fully accepted as an element in the program evaluator's professional role, the unresponsiveness of knowledge utilization barriers to passive communication strategies seems to require evaluators at least to become more actively involved in the interpretation and use of the results of their findings. The evaluation reports of the future may have sections like the following:

> Treatment B was found to be marginally superior to Treatment A on most outcome measures, and it is likely that Treatment A will have the same client utilization as Treatment B (i.e., one half of all clients will drop out in the first two weeks, and two thirds of those remaining will complete the full course of therapy.)

> While Treatment X was superior to Treatment Y on all outcome and consumer satisfaction measures, Treatment X is incompatible with the values and philosophies of most practitioners in this field, and when used in clinical settings may be so modified as to render the results of this evaluation inapplicable.

> Evaluation System C meets the technical requirements of curreng legislation and costs about the same as comparable systems. Installation of the system requires extensive staff retraining however, supplemented by periodic refresher sessions. In the absence of such continued support, the staff skills necessary to maintain the evaluation will decay and in a few years the evaluation system will erode into a nearly unrecognizable replica of the original.

If these forecasts are correct, future consumers of evaluation research will routinely expect recommendations on how to make use of findings, and in the absence of such recommendations will ask, "Where is the change analysis?"

REFERENCES

BARNETT, H. G. (1953) Innovation: The Basis of Cultural Change. New York: McGraw-Hill.

BECKER, S. W. and T. L. WHISLER (1967) "The innovative organization: a selective view of current theory and research." Journal of Business 40: 462-469.

BONOMA, T. V. (1977) "Overcoming resistance to changes recommended for operating programs." Professional Psychology (November): 451-463.

CALSYN, R., L. TORNATZKY, and S. DITTMAR (1977) "Incomplete adoption of innovation: The case of goal attainment scaling." Evaluation, 4: 127-130.

CAMPBELL, D. T. (1972) "Reforms as experiments," in C. H. Weiss (ed.) Evaluating Action Programs: Readings in Social Action and Education. Boston: Allyn and Bacon.

CAPLAN, N. (1975) "The use of social science information by federal executives," in G. Lyons (ed.) Social Research and Public Policies: The Dartmouth/OECD Conference. Hanover, NH: Dartmouth College.

CHIN, R. and K. D. BENNE (1969) "General strategies for effecting change in human systems," in W. G. Bennis, K. D. Benne and R. Chin (eds.) The Planning of Change. New York: Holt, Rinehart and Winston.

COLEMAN, J. S., E. KATZ, and H. MENZEL (1966) Medical Innovation: A Diffusion Study. Indianapolis: Bobbs-Merrill.

DAVIS, H. R. (1973) "Change and innovation," in S. Feldman (ed.) Administration and Mental Health. Springfield, IL: Charles C. Thomas.

——— and S. E. SALASIN (1975) "Improving the policy relevance of social research and development, in L. Lynn (ed.) National Academy of Sciences Study Project on Social Research and Development. Washington, DC: National Academy of Sciences.

FAIRWEATHER, G. W., D. H. SANDERS, and L. G. TORNATZKY (1974) Creating Change in Mental Health Organizations. New York: Pergamon.

FLIEGEL, F. C. and J. E. KIVLIN (1966) "Attributes of innovations as factors in diffusion." American Journal of Sociology 72(3): 235-248.

GIANNETTI, R. A., J. H. JOHNSON, and T. A. WILLIAMS (1978) "Computer technology in community mental health centers: Current status and future prospects." Unpublished paper, Norfolk, Virginia: Eastern Virginia Medical School.

GLASER, E. M. (1973) "Knowledge transfer and institutional change." Professional Psychology 4: 434-444.

——— and T. BACKER (1977) "Innovation redefined: durability and local adoption." Evaluation 4: 131-135.

GLASER, E. M. and J. B. MARKS (1966) "Putting research to work." Rehabilitation Record 7,6: 6-10.

HAGE, J. and M. AIKEN (1970) Social Change in Complex Organizations. New York: Random House.

HAVELOCK, R. (1969) Planning for Innovation Through Dissemination and Utilization of Knowledge. Ann Arbor: Center for Research on Utilization of Scientific Knowledge, Institute for Social Research, University of Michigan.

——— (1968) "Dissemination and translation roles," in T. L. Eidell and J. M. Kitchel (eds.) Knowledge Production and Utilization in Educational Administration. Eugene, OR: Center for the Advanced Study of Educational Administration, University of Oregon.

——— and D. A. LINGWOOD (1973) R & D Utilization Strategies and Functions: An Analytical Comparison of Four Systems. Ann Arbor: Institute for Social Research, University of Michigan.

HOVELAND, C. I., I. L. JANIS, and H. H. KELLEY (1953) Communication and Persuasion. New Haven, CT: Yale Univ. Press.

Human Interaction Research Institute (1976) Putting Knowledge To Use: A Distillation of the Literature Regarding Knowledge Transfer and Change. Los Angeles: Author.

JOLY, J. (1967) "Research and innovation: two solitudes?" Canadian Education and Research Digest 2: 184-194.

KATZ, E., M. L. LEVIN, and H. HAMILTON (1963) "Traditions of research on the diffusion of innovations." American Sociological Review 28, 2: 237-252.

KIRESUK, T. J., H. DAVIS, and S. LUND (in press) "Knowledge transfer and planned change in mental health care delivery systems," in J. Sidowski, J. Johnson, and T. Williams (eds.) Technology in Mental Health Care Delivery Systems. Norwood, NJ: Ablex.

KIRESUK, T. J. and S. H. LUND (in press) "Goal attainment scaling: a medical-correctional application," in C. Roy (ed.) Perspectives in Prison Psychiatry. Oxford, England: Oxford Univ. Press.

KIRESUK, T. J. and R. E. SHERMAN (1968) "Goal attainment scaling: a general method for evaluating comprehensive community mental health programs." Community Mental Health Journal 4: 443-453.

KNORR, K. D. (1977) "Policymakers' use of social science knowledge: symbolic or instrumental?" in C. Weiss (ed.) Using Social Research in Public Policy Making. Lexington, MA: Lexington Books.

LARSEN, J. (1978a) "Utilization of policy-oriented evaluation: a comparative study." Presented at Evaluation Research Society, Washington, DC.

——— (1978b) Adoption of New Knowledge in Mental Health Services. Progress report to National Institute of Mental Health, grant No. R12 MH 25121. American Institutes for Research, Palo Alto, California.

——— and R. AGARWALA-ROGERS (1977) "Re-invention of innovative ideas: modified? adopted? none of the above?" Evaluation 4: 136-140.

LEWIN, K. (1962) "Quasi-stationary social equilibria and the problem of permanent change," in W. G. Bennis, K. D. Benne and R. Chin (eds.) The Planning of Change: Readings in the Applied Sciences. New York: Holt, Rinehart & Winston.

LIPPITT, R. O. and R. FOX (1967) Identifying, Documenting, Evaluating and Sharing Innovative Classroom Practices. Washington, DC: Office of Education, U.S. Department of Health, Education and Welfare.

MANSFIELD, E. (1963) "The speed of response of firms to new techniques." Quarterly Journal of Economics 77, 2: 290-311.

MAYER, S. E. (1975) "The organizational readiness to accept program evaluation questionnaire: scoring and interpretation." PERC Newsletter 6, 6.

MILES, M. B. (1965) "Planned change and organizational health: figure and ground," in R. O. Carlson et al., Change Processes in the Public Schools. Eugene, OR: Center for the Advanced Study of Educational Administration, University of Oregon.

MOHR, L. B. (1969) "Determinants of innovations in organizations." American Political Science Review 63: 111-126.

MUSHKIN, S. J. (1973) "Evaluations: use with caution." Evaluation 1, 2: 30-36.

MYTINGER, R. E. (1968) "Innovations in local health services," in Public Health Service, Division of Medical Care Administration. Arlington, VA: U.S. Department of Health, Education and Welfare.

National Science Foundation (1973) Science, Technology and Innovation. (Report on Contract No. NSF - C667). Columbus, OH: Battelle Columbus Laboratories.

PATTON, M. (1978) Utilization-Focused Evaluation. Beverly Hills: Sage Publications.

RICH, R. F. (1977) "Use of social science information by federal bureaucrats: knowledge for action versus knowledge for understanding," in C. Weiss (ed.) Using Social Research in Public Policy Making. Lexington, MA: Lexington Books.

ROGERS, E. M. (1962) Diffusion of Innovations. New York: Free Press.

——— and F. F. SHOEMAKER (1971) Communication of Innovations: A Cross-Cultural Approach. New York: Free Press.

ROSSI, P. H., H. E. FREEMAN, and S. R. WRIGHT (1979) Evaluation: A Systematic Approach. Beverly Hills: Sage Publications.

ROTHMAN, J. (1974) Planning and Organizing for Social Change: Action Principles from Social Science Research. New York: Columbia Univ. Press.

SALASIN, S. E. and H. R. DAVIS (1977) "Facilitating the utilization of evaluation: a rocky road," in I. Davidoff, M. Guttentag, and J. Offutt (eds.) Evaluating Community Mental Health Services. Rockville, MD: National Institute of Mental Health.

SASHKIN, M., W. MORRIS , and L. HORST (1973) "A comparison of social and organizational change models: information flow and data use processes." Psychological Review 80, 6: 510-526.

SCRIVEN, M. (1974) "Exploring goal free evaluation: an interview with Michael Scriven" (Susan Salasin, interviewer). Evaluation 2, 1.

——— (1972) "The methodology of evaluation," in C. Weiss (ed.) Evaluating Social Action Programs: Readings in Social Action and Education. Boston: Allyn and Bacon.

SPICER, E. H. [ed.] (1952) Human Problems in Technological Change: A Casebook. New York: Russell Sage.

STROMMEN, M. (1978) Effecting Utilization: Experimental Use of Consultants. Report to the National Institute of Mental Health, Grant No. R01 MH28498. Minneapolis, MN: Search Institute.

STUDER, S. L. (1978) "A validity study of a measure of 'readiness for evaluation.'" Ph.D. dissertation, University of Minnesota.

THOMPSON, M. (1954) The Cry and the Covenant. New York: Doubleday.

WEISS, C. (1972) "Utilization of evaluation: toward comparative study," in C. Weiss (ed.) Evaluating Social Action Programs: Readings in Social Action and Education. Boston: Allyn and Bacon.

WHOLEY, J. S. (1977) "Evaluability assessment," in L. Rutman (ed.) Evaluation Research: A Basic Guide. Beverly Hills: Sage Publications.

ZALTMAN, G. and R. DUNCAN (1977) Strategies for Planned Change. New York: John Wiley.

——— and J. HOLBEK (1973) Innovations and Organizations. New York: John Wiley.

Robert Perloff
University of Pittsburgh

4

EVALUATOR INTERVENTION
The Case For and Against

Originally, I had planned to focus upon the need for theory in evaluation as the theme for my Evaluation Research Society presidential address, but a funny thing happened on my way to this forum. An incident arose in connection with the National Institute of Education grant (more about which, below) to ERS which suggested strongly to me that as important as theory may be in the long run for the flowering and viability of evaluation research and even for program evaluation, of even greater importance for success and credibility is, in my judgment, a whole series of questions, problems, concerns, and controversies which arise in our everyday execution of evaluation studies. One of these concerns—or at least it is a concern to me—is the matter of the evaluator's intrusion or intervention into the program whose conduct and outcomes he or she is evaluating. This intervention may frequently and perhaps more often than not be salutary, benign, and constructive, as in fact may be the case in the situation I shall describe below, but it is not unlikely that in a given evaluation inquiry the evaluation of a program may be imperiled or corrupted by the evaluator's intrusion, an intrusion no matter how well intended. Because of the natural

AUTHOR'S NOTE: *This is a modified version of the author's presidential address delivered at the Second Annual Meeting of the Evaluation Research Society, November 2, 1978, Washington, DC.*

tendency for sensitive human beings—and evaluators are indisputably sensitive and caring people—to want to make things come out right, an inclination facing us all as we engage in evaluation undertakings, and because, as Robert Burns said a long time ago (and it is valid today), "the best laid plans of mice and men gang aft aglay," I decided that this phenomenon of evaluator intervention, both its pro and con aspects, was a more urgent problem to address by us in the Evaluation Research Society than the more glamorous though less immediately useful topic of theory. Before considering the matter of evaluator intervention directly, let me first put this activity in the context of the Evaluation Research Society (ERS) grant awarded by the National Institute of Education (NIE).

THE ERS GRANT

Toward the end of Marcia Guttentag's ERS presidency a grant was negotiated between the Evaluation Research Society (through Harvard University, where Guttentag was located at that time) and the National Institute of Education. The purpose of this grant was to advise NIE and another one of its grantees AIR (American Institutes for Research), in the conduct of an evaluation of a program called "Cities in School." NIE viewed ERS's advisory role as serving two purposes. First, as an arm, of sorts, both of NIE and of AIR, to provide counsel to NIE and AIR in the design and conduct of the "Cities in School" evaluation by AIR, counsel intended to complement and reinforce AIR's capabilities in evaluation research. Second, ERS's participation was aimed at developing a kind of model for providing technical counsel to federal agencies and their contractors and grantees for subsequent evaluation studies, where by "model" I do not at all mean that, necessarily, ERS would be the grantee, but that some outside or "third party" group or panel would serve in such an advisory capacity should the ERS-NIE-AIR experience prove valuable and workable.

When Marcia Guttentag died, the ERS Council authorized me to serve in her place as principal investigator for this grant.

It is thus incumbent upon me to inform you about this grant and then about this intervention phenomenon constituting the core of this paper. But first I must acquaint you (1) with the "Cities in School" program itself and (2) with the AIR evaluation enterprise.

CITIES IN SCHOOL

"Cities in School" (CIS) is an experimental program—hence the need and the mandate to evaluate it—for deprived youngsters, and is now in operation experimentally in Atlanta, Indianapolis, and New York, and mention has been made of the possibility that "Cities in School" will soon be operating in the District of Columbia. "Cities in School" was allotted nearly two-and-a-quarter million dollars in 1978 in grants from a number of federal agencies and is reportedly in line for around the same level of funding for at least one succeeding year.

CIS is a program designed to integrate the delivery of a variety of social and educational services to inner-city students (in the three aforementioned cities) and their families. It is contended by CIS advocates that extant procedures for helping inner-city youth have not been particularly successful, judging from the fact that a large number of these intended beneficiaries of these welfare programs are "stuck in the no-skill/unemployment/welfare cycle that they have grown up with." It has been hypothesized that the existing system duplicates some services and neglects others, where "The client is not treated as a whole person, but as a bundle of discrete problems to be addressed in isolation . . . a teenager living in poverty, without one or both parents, failing school, possibly pregnant, thinking about dropping out, needs help with several interrelated and interdependent problems. Treating them separately, as the traditional system does, is seldom effective."

Another fundamental barrier inherent in the current service delivery system as CIS views it, is "*access* to the people who need the services. In the existing system, the initiative rests to an unreasonable degree with the recipient. He or she must recognize the problem, learn about the service, find out where it can be obtained, travel to an unfamiliar place to seek help from strangers, and then, too often, have to deal with an indifferent or obstructive bureaucrat. For many people who need the service, the option of doing nothing is simply much easier to take."

As the result of the present system, therefore, and to sum up the defects that CIS is hoping to overcome, current efforts to help these inner-city young people are hampered by a lack of coordination, a lack of personalism, a lack of accountability (no one is held responsible for failure or rewarded for success), and a lack of morale (both client and staff get discouraged by lack of results). For these reasons, then, "CIS has taken as its objective to see that the services are placed together, brought to the client, integrated to deal with the client as a whole person, and put on a personal level based on a primary one-to-one relationship." The two distinguishing features of CIS are (1) using the school as the hub for service delivery and (2) the breadth of services combined and offered.

This, then, in a nutshell is the kernel of the CIS idea. I will not burden you now with the structural features of CIS in its three cities, the similarities and differences among CIS as it is in place in these three cities, nor with the nomenclature—for example, youth coordinators, programmatic specialists, social service workers, supportive educators, caseloads, caseload managers, and the notion of "family"—indigenous to CIS, but suffice it to say that "Cities in School" is a comprehensive, thoughtful, and systematic approach toward the improvement of the effectiveness of a variety of services for disadvantaged elements in the school population.

THE AIR EVALUATION

Inherent in CIS are efforts to demonstrate the validity of four assertions:

(1) CIS provides a superior structure and a process for integrated service delivery to disadvantaged youngsters;

(2) the higher quality of service leads to significant, positive impact on the youth;

(3) these positive benefits can be achieved without an excessive increase in the cost of present alternative delivery systems (which produce less benefit); and

(4) CIS is a feasible model for adoption by other cities (beyond Atlanta, Indianapolis, and New York) to replace their current system.

The foregoing four assertions constitute the basis for the essential questions that the evaluation will address:

(1) What are the effects of CIS on the youth it serves?

(2) What are the effects of CIS on the quality of service?

(3) Is the CIS program progressing toward institutionalization?

(4) What are the costs of CIS?

The ERS technical review panel has met with NIE and AIR personnel on three occasions. In January 1978 we met at one of the sites of CIS, Indianapolis. In April 1978 we met in New Orleans, and in August 1978 we met at Asilomar, California. Other meetings are planned.

The technical review panel consists of Ward Edwards, Gene Glass, Malcolm Klein, Robert Stake, Eugene Webb, David Wiley, and me. Four or five of us have met with AIR personnel and the NIE project manager, Norman Gold, on each of the three meetings convened to date. Additionally, telephone conversations and an exchange of reports following the three meetings have provided what to me is an impressive set of recommendations for evaluating and reacting to the AIR design.

Let me now proceed to the matter of intervention, skipping a recitation of the variables that AIR has included in its evaluation, consideration of control and comparison groups, experimental design, and the like, all of which are matters of record.

"THE EVALUATOR'S FAMILIAR REFRAIN"

In preparing for the ERS Technical Review Panel's meeting with AIR and NIE at Asilomar in early August, AIR shared with the panel several observations vis-a-vis the CIS enterprise and how it was progressing:

(1) Only about half of the youngsters came into the program with the kinds of behavioral problems that the program expected to find;

(2) only a minority of the case managers accept the kind of accountability for the whole youngster—the "holistic approach"—that is the centerpiece of the CIS rhetoric;

(3) service integration on an institutional level is not occurring, except in the most isolated instances; and

(4) when the approach is implemented as planned, for students who have the problems that were expected, CIS may be doing quite well.

This is the "evaluator's familiar refrain." AIR advised the panel that the promise of CIS might become obscured by major discrepancies between what the program was intended to be and what it actually is. "But the promise of the program remains seductive. When it works, it really works." The question was raised, in view of the above problems which could well invalidate the CIS concept, whether succeeding evaluation phases should be undertaken. And it turned out that it was this question which occupied the lion's share of the time we spent at Asilomar. Interwoven with this question was the matter of intervention or intrusion into the operational program. How and to what extent should we seek to judiciously advise CIS personnel about the ways the CIS structure might be modified so as to more faithfully resemble the original CIS rhetoric, rhetoric which, I might add, is what in effect AIR had agreed to evaluate and which we, ERS, agreed to comment upon in our advisory/consultative/review roles. Before raising my own issues and questions vis-a-vis intervention per se, let me first summarize for you the flavor of the diversity of opinions of the panel itself, with respect to this intervention issue.

A COLLAGE OF THE PANEL'S VIEWS
ON EVALUATOR INTERVENTION

One panelist suggested that "since the preliminary AIR findings show the nonexistence of the program as advertised, it is appropriate to intervene and hope to help create the program AIR is commissioned to evaluate. . . . But to take this line runs heavy risks, particularly to the ability to generalize to other programs. It is this point, the external validity one, that causes me most concern with the argument that one must make sure that a phenomenon exists before it can be evaluated or measured. Without external validity, one engages in journalism. However interesting that journalism may be, it offers us little to learn from."

Another panelist distinguished among three objectives of evaluation: (1) the conceptual entity or the rhetoric of the program; (2) the methods of implementation of a program; and (3) the impact of the program. Concerning the second objective, methods of implementation, he observed that "Evaluation of this is made more difficult by the fact that unfavorable evaluation of an effort at implementation will of course lead to an attempt to improve that implementation. The evaluation is in effect looking at a process, rather than at a set of results. In my opinion, such feedback from evaluation to implementation effort is both inevitable and perfectly appropriate; indeed, it is one of the most important advantages of performing any kind of evaluation." So this panelist comes down on the side of favoring some kind of intervention by the evaluator, on the basis that it is a myth that the evaluator or any observer or experimenter, for that matter, does not affect the phenomena he or she is observing. Science is not value-free, nor is the scientist. If you can help make a model you are evaluating more "evaluatable," if you will, then there is no harm in doing this. Good science, according to this argument, is done not only in the laboratory, but also in the field; conditions in the field will oftentimes justify *formative* intervention, from the point of view of program development and refinement.

Still another panelist was eclectic on the issue of intervention. His stance "on the issue of the proper level of researcher intrusion varies from project to project on the basis of stated goals and level of implementation achieved." Concerning CIS in particular, this panelist adopted the following posture:

(1) The AIR data and impressions are sufficient to determine that CIS has not been implemented sufficiently to provide a valid test of its conceptual structure;

(2) CIS is unique; major modifications or failures at implementation will damage its unique character so much as to change that character into that of "just another" intense service delivery system, of which there have been many;

(3) most special projects which have been independently and carefully evaluated have seemed to be failures (in terms of youth impact), but often have not been implemented sufficiently that their idea systems can be shown to be related to the failures (i.e., the "serum level" wasn't high enough);

(4) we shouldn't bother doing major evaluations (as this one is) on nonunique projects.

This panelist then suggested that we have three choices to make. "We can abandon ship and watch her sink; we can stay close by, with a reduced evaluation effort sufficient to document the struggle to keep the ship afloat; or we can feed in the data, and force the issues that will not only keep the ship afloat, but make it look like the vessel she was supposed to be." He opted for the last position, but for the next six months only, at the end of which time a decision "can reasonably be made about continuation." He proposed that a conceptual model (the CIS rhetoric) should lead to program activities (which has not been satisfactorily the case with CIS), which in turn should lead to impact. He argued that if impact measurements were taken at this time, they would reflect not the original model or the program activities stemming from that model, but rather an alternative model and a lesser program which he labeled as a "fall-back position." He thought that it would be an error to evaluate fall-back positions which in effect severely restricted the original (rhetoric) propositions. He concluded that we should "give the original propositions a chance to demonstrate their validity even if we have to help the practitioners implement their own practice."

Finally, I should like to recapitulate for you the views of a fourth panelist. He remained

concerned about the amount of intervention which the evaluation team may take. It is clear that there are departures from the grand conceptualization of the program. It is not clear that the evaluation team has the responsibility, or the insight, for suggesting better directions the project might take. . . . My experience with federal program evaluation . . . is that well intending, well trained technical specialists are usually more disruptive than facilitative as they point out weaknesses in operation, especially when it relates to information processing. They too often presume that the same kind of information that fits into a good evaluation is information that makes the program people more aware and better able. . . . They are reluctant to admit how low the quality of their information is, and thus imply that their advice is based more soundly than it is. They sometimes seem to disrupt the program with admonitions for improvement knowing that they will get changes which will invalidate their evaluation design, and maybe excuse them from getting no better findings than they end up with. . . . I do not know of a single case where there is willful disruptiveness by evaluators, but intent is not necessary for negative influence to occur. . . . I do not know how to deal with [the] plea that we help the program people out. I believe that you have to go by your contract. . . . You have to observe professional ethics and the methods and expectations of your colleagues. All those press you to refuse to provide information if it would alter the course of the program. . . . Informally you have promised feedback, so you have that obligation to assist. It is conceivable that you could provide them with something important they do not know, or even give them an opportunity to admit something they have not. I think it unlikely. If I felt that you really could help them I would not push for abstinence. I have doubts. . . . I do not mean to say that I think we should avoid talking to them. I think we should tell them some of the impressions we have, and even share some of the more dependable data, but I think that we should insist that we doubt if our interpretations are as good as their own, at least at this point.

This panelist, along with the other panel members, including me, is supportive of the effort by and of the competence of the evaluation design and the evaluation to date. His views and those of the rest of us simply represent the variety of perceptions of a terribly complex evaluation of an "untidy" program such as CIS, but then again I would ask the question whether any program is really tidy and if it is tidy then it probably is not particularly important. But before leaving CIS, NIE, AIR, and ERS, let me share with you briefly an example of a situation where the evaluator's values might in fact get in the way of a reasonably objective and valid evaluation. One of our panelists was commenting upon an internal AIR memorandum wherein the writer of that memorandum thoughtfully, sincerely, with good intentions, and some will probably even say with a measure of validity, lamented that a "missed opportunity" on the part of CIS personnel was not to promote uniform teaching methods, concerning which the panelist suggests that if the evaluator is prejudiced in favor of uniform teaching methods, then perhaps that evaluator cannot evaluate the situation. "This seems to me," one panelist declared, to be "an instance where the evaluator's yearning for uniformity (as principle or just because things might be understandable then) gets in the way of reporting and judging the quality of effort."

THE CASE FOR EVALUATOR INTERVENTION

One matter is reasonably clear to me. Aside from the advantages and disadvantages of evaluator intrusion, the costs and benefits of such behavior, and propriety or impropriety of intervention, it is an indisputably crucial issue that demands our attention. Under what conditions should intrusion be countenanced? What should the intruder's qualifications be? What are the ethics underlying intrusion or, for that matter, can a case be made for the proposition that in certain circumstances *not* to intrude is unethical more or less in the same vein that it is said that if one stays aloof from a problem or from problem definition (which some might characterize as process or formative evaluation) one must bear the responsibility for something less than an optimal solution to the problem. While I have not examined the literature on this exhaustively, I am confident that save for skirting around the edges of the problem in terms of ethics in evaluation, the values of the evaluator, the pros and cons of external versus internal evaluations, the politics of evaluation, and the like, the issue of evaluator intervention has not been empirically or, for that matter, suggestively or speculatively addressed. What I am hoping to stimulate in this chapter is some concern in the evaluation community, some dialogue, and some factual, empirical, field consideration, an experiment perhaps, scrutinizing systematically and comprehensively the nature and consequences of evaluator intervention.

From a positive point of view, a case can clearly be made for evaluator intervention, in terms of the contention that in terms of process or formative evaluation, intervention is not at all inappropriate, or in terms of the reasoned position that if a phenomenon which the evaluator was designated to evaluate is not present in the first place then the evaluator may be obliged to contribute toward the shaping of that phenomenon rather than unsatisfactorily and incompletely retreating to the evaluation of a "fall-back" position.

From a humanistic point of view, one might adopt the laudable posture that it would be a waste of effort and a threat to the welfare of this or that target population were evaluators to antiseptically or heartlessly, in the name of "objectivity" or of "pure science," abandon the welfare of that target population in deference to a mindless adherence to the false god of scientism and to an "arms length" attitude toward real people who are hungry, in pain, or otherwise deprived or disadvantaged.

THE CASE AGAINST
EVALUATOR INTERVENTION

Let me say first that I certainly agree with the proposition that one should take one case at a time. One cannot and should not condemn all interventions as improper or sanction in a wholesale way all interventions. Let me say too that, probably, some modest and judicious intervention in the CIS operation would be fitting. Let me say too that I do not believe that in a knee-jerk fashion one should say that he or she who favors intervention is necessarily a humanist on the side of "doing good" and that necessarily he or she who opposes intervention is deserving of being called a reactionary or labeled as insensitive to the needs of people and communities who need help. The cause of—trite as it sounds—pursuing "truth" can only be impaired by engaging in this kind of thoughtless name calling or stereotyping.

Having said this let me make my own emerging—emerging, I repeat, and not definitive or conclusive, or final—position. I tilt toward nonintervention. Other things equal, I would caution against intervention by the evalutor, *by the evaluator* I must add. I am not against intervention, obviously, by experienced operational people intimately knowledgable about the program, nor am I opposed to—for in fact I vigorously favor—intervention following the completion of a tried-and-true evaluation showing that a particular program works, essentially the position espoused by the preceding chapter in this volume.

Several arguments might be forwarded in opposition to evaluator intervention of the sort we have been discussing. One of these is the threat to external validity. That is, to what extent will we be able to generalize the results of an evaluation, positive or negative, if the operational nature of the program was clearly influenced by people, evaluators in this instance, whose presence for similar influence, for good or ill, could not be assured in the operational phase of the program once it has been evaluated? For example, with respect to the CIS program, and this is given only as an example of what can happen and does not at all suggest that it will happen in CIS, consider perhaps the kind of counsel that an evaluator might give the operational people: do a better job of selecting youngsters for the program; have the case managers do a better job of working with youngsters, for example, working with them at home as well as in school; or do this or that to enhance service integration in the school. Now, if it turns out that such benign tampering turns a program around so that once it has transcended its experimental stage and is operating out in the field, its actual operation is a mirror of what took place in the experimental program so influenced by the evaluator, then this is all well and good. The question arises, however, whether the kind of influence exerted experimentally could reasonably be expected to become manifest in the field. I have serious doubts about this, very serious doubts. One might go still further and suggest that if a program, again using CIS as an example and not as a whipping boy, is such—its politics, the nature of commitment or lack thereof by case managers, and the like—that the original model, the original rhetoric, simply cannot be implemented, that the "nature of the beast" is such that it cannot be done, then the evaluator who tampers is perpetrating a very expensive Type I error that will, at the same time, drain off funds that might more effectively be used for a program which does work or which can be shown to work.

A not unrelated additional problem I have with this kind of intervention has to do with the competence of an evaluator to make suggestions or recommendations bearing upon a substantive matter dealing with service delivery per se as opposed to evaluation procedures and strategies.

Third, the effect of experimenter bias has been documented again and again, notwithstanding some flaws in earlier studies probing the phenomenon. The experimenter who expects his or her subjects to respond in certain ways is more likely to obtain those responses than the experimenter with no such prior expectations, the point being, placed in the evaluation context, that the evaluator who quite earnestly and with the best of intentions recommends program changes, may a la self-fulfilling prophecy, observe that the changes he or she recommended actually "worked out," where "worked out" is in quotation marks. Jones (1977: 107) attributes to Baker and Crist the suggestion that "the question for future research is not whether there are expectancy effects, but how they operate." In the context of our present concern, this admonition cannot be overemphasized and is a concern underscoring my own anxiety over the ultimately harmful effects of evaluator intervention.

Let me continue. In a seminal review by Wells (1978), the evidence shows clearly that (1) "helping professionals perceive more pathology in a given target than do lay persons," (2) "helpers' perceptions of a given client are consistently less favorable than lay persons' perceptions, irrespective of whether the target person is normal or psychologically impaired," and (3) "helpers rate clients substantially less favorably than they rate themselves, for dimensions including general evaluation as well as problem-solving capability." The point of all this is that, as I view the world, it is not unreasonable to expect that evaluators, not unlike their service delivery colleagues actually involved in giving treatment, may see people as being less well, less bright, less able to cope, less well adjusted, and so forth, than themselves (the evaluators) and that, therefore, the clients need to be helped, come hell or high water. It might turn out that in some instances the values of evaluators (along with their possibly patronizing attitude toward clients or populations for which remedial programs are being evaluated) could well induce these clients or populations into behaving in ways which they believe the evaluators expect the clients or populations to behave.

All of this suggests, though it does not convince me beyond the shadow of a doubt, that we should be wary about evaluator intervention, which is not to say that it should be counseled against in all situations, only that its effects need to be pondered.

Program advocates to not qualify as program evaluators by dint of their status as program advocates and similarly program evaluators ought not to be viewed as being qualified as program managers or as specialists in treatment delivery; specialists in *determining the effectiveness of treatment*, yes, but not in *delivering the treatment*.

Intervention should indisputably occur after an evaluation has shown that the program works and then intervention enters the arena of knowledge utilization, after it has been demonstrated that treatment is effective.

Perhaps one way to avoid the dilemma facing the evaluation task in the CIS program is to have more smaller scale or pilot studies. Spend less money, involve fewer communities and fewer people, and then if problems emerge, they can be worked out in the pilot or seed study, so that the rhetoric or model will be given a fair chance once the kinks have been ironed out.

Compassionate people—and evaluators are compassionate—cannot help but strive to modify programs they are asked to evaluate. Evaluators may be especially heedful, I am confident, to their inner urges to intervene when not to intervene will give them the disquieting feeling that if they do not intrude, a program will go down the drain and with it the opportunity to better the human condition. Maybe so, but the other side of the coin is that intrusion may well-nigh do no good, at best, or at worst intrusion may deflect sorely needed resources from a program whose promise is far greater than the one that the evaluator feels obliged to salvage.

REFERENCES

BAKER, J. P. and J. L. CRIST (1971) Teacher expectancies: a review of the literature," in J. D. Elashoff and R. E. Snow (eds.) Pygmalion Reconsidered. Worthington, OH: Charles A. Jones.

JONES, R. A. (1977) Self-Fulfilling Prophecies: Social, Psychological and Physiological Effects of Expectancies. Hillsdale, NJ: Lawrence Erlbaum.

WELLS, T. A. (1978) "Perceptions of clients by professional helpers." Psychological Bulletin 5: 968-1000.

ABOUT THE AUTHORS

WARD EDWARDS is Director of the Social Science Research Institute and Professor of Psychology and of Industrial & Systems Engineering at USC. The institute conducts large-scale research programs applying scientific tools and methods to problems such as evaluation and improvement of criminal justice systems, dispute resolution policy, biosocial studies of the etiology of schizophrenia and criminality, use of geographically coded records for social program evaluation, differential-equation models of social phenomena, and the like. Dr. Edwards is a psychologist by training, and his personal research interests are mainly decision analysis, behavior decision theory, and Bayesian ideas. His current research is mostly concerned with characteristics of multiattribute utility models, elicitation methods appropriate to their use, and especially the use of such models in the evaluation of complex real entities. In 1978, he won the Franklin V. Taylor Award of the Society of Engineering Psychologists.

THOMAS J. KIRESUK is Chief Clinical Psychologist at Hennepin County Medical Center in Minneapolis, Minnesota. He is also Director of the Program Evaluation Resource Center (PERC), a research and dissemination project funded by the Mental Health Services Development Branch of the National Institute of Mental Health, and chief editorial reviewer for *Evaluation and Change* magazine. He holds a doctorate in clinical psychology from the University of Minnesota, and is a clinical professor in the university's graduate school and a professor in the medical school's department of psychiatry. He has published many articles on program evaluation, research utilization, and planned change, and maintains memberships in many professional organizations. Dr. Kiresuk is a 1979 recipient of the Evaluation Research Society's Myrdal Prize.

SANDER H. LUND is Associate Director of PERC and has also served as an evaluation consultant to a variety of human service organizations. He holds a bachelor's degree from the University of Minnesota and is working toward a masters degree in sociology from Mankato State University.

ROBERT PERLOFF is formerly Director of Research and Development for Science Research Associates, Inc., and Director of Research Programs at the Graduate School of business of the University of Pittsburgh. He is currently Professor of Business Administration and of Psychology at the University of Pittsburgh. He has published and presented papers widely in applied social science, particularly in evaluation research, measurement and statistics, consumer research, and organizational behavior. Professor Perloff is Past-President of the Evaluation Research Society as well as of the Association for Consumer Research, and at present time is Treasurer and a member of the Board of Directors of the American Psychological Association, and a member of the Board of Directors of the Eastern Psychological Association.

ROBERT E. STAKE is Professor of Educational Psychology and Director of the Center for Instructional Research and Curriculum Evaluation at the University of Illinois at Urbana-Champaign. He is a specialist in program evaluation who emphasizes naturalistic research and a "responsive" approach to the evaluation of educational activities. Recently he directed a national study of elementary and secondary school science teaching and learning using a case study approach. The sponsor was the National Science Foundation. His recent work also includes environmental education, museum programs, youth transition from school to work, and teacher education.